Research Report No. 20

OPERATIONAL AUDITS OF PRODUCTION CONTROL

by Gary L. Holstrum, PhD, CPA, and William A. Collins, PhD, CPA

THE INSTITUTE OF INTERNAL AUDITORS, INC.

ISBN 0-89413-056-0
Library of Congress Catalog Card Number 77-080966

IIA 77099-Jan78
IIA 82006-Jan82

FOREWORD

The production control function is responsible for determining that material, labor, and machines are available to produce the optimum production quantity to meet customer needs. To meet this responsibility effectively, the production control function must judiciously allocate major resource expenditures.

The audit of the production control function provides internal auditors with an opportunity to assist members of management by furnishing them with analyses, appraisals, recommendations, and pertinent comments concerning this activity.

This research report is designed to provide internal auditors and others with a practical framework for reviewing the production control function. The experiences of those who took part in the research fieldwork should provide valuable information on the various methods used by practitioners in fulfilling their responsibilities.

The Institute of Internal Auditors expresses its appreciation to all those whose individual contributions have resulted in the publishing of *Operational Audits of Production Control.* We also wish to thank the project researchers and the International Research Committee's project manager, Gilbert C. Hogue, whose interest and dedication contributed so much to the successful completion of this project.

James R. Kelly, CIA
1977-78 International President

ACKNOWLEDGMENTS

The research described in this report resulted from the efforts of many people. Although it is not possible to identify all the contributors, we wish to express special appreciation to some of them.

We are especially grateful to William Perry, director of professional practice for The Institute, and to Gilbert C. Hogue, chairman of IIA's Research Subcommittee for this project. They provided essential counsel, direction, coordination, and continual support throughout the project. Significant editorial help was provided by Pete Warner, IIA's assistant manager of professional standards, and by members of the Research Subcommittee: Robert P. Logue, William H. Sachau, and C. W. Gissel.

During field visits to firms, many individuals provided valuable suggestions, audit programs, and audit reports on production control. Especially valuable help was provided by Don J. Whittingham, The Warner & Swasey Co.; Stanley Gross and Ralph Weir, The Sherwin-Williams Co.; Ed McNulty, G. D. Searle & Co.; William B. Costill, Harris Corporation; Dick Loechler, The General Tire & Rubber Co.; Chris Wilhelm and Dennis Michaelson of Xerox; and by Decio Gaeta and Ray Karsh of ITT.

Our research efforts were also aided considerably by the representatives of numerous firms who responded to our questionnaire and provided descriptions of the production control systems and problems in their firms.

William A. Collins, PhD, CPA
Gary L. Holstrum, PhD, CPA
December 1977

PROJECT RESEARCHERS

Gary L. Holstrum, PhD, CPA, and William A. Collins, PhD, CPA, are faculty members of the Accounting Department at the University of Florida. Their primary areas of interest are auditing and financial reporting.

Holstrum presently serves as an advisor to the Auditing Standards Executive Committee of the American Institute of Certified Public Accountants, a member and former chairman of the Continuing Education Committee, and a member of the Committee on Education of the American Accounting Association. In addition, Holstrum's papers have appeared in the *Journal of Accounting Research, The Accounting Review, Journal of Accountancy,* and *Management Accounting.*

Collins served as a seminar leader on Production Control at the 35th International Conference of Internal Auditors held in Boston in June 1976.

Both are actively involved in the continuing education program sponsored by the Florida Institute of Certified Public Accountants. They serve as seminar leaders and, with Charles L. McDonald, coauthored texts for continuing education seminars in auditing and accounting. Holstrum and Collins are also coauthors of "Internal Audits of Production Control Adaptiveness" which appeared in *The Internal Auditor* in December 1976.

THE INSTITUTE OF INTERNAL AUDITORS
INTERNATIONAL RESEARCH COMMITTEE
1977-1978

CONTENTS

FIGURES

1 INTRODUCTION

The production control function is responsible for determining that material, labor, and machines are available to produce the optimum production quantity to meet customer needs based on sales forecasts. Thus, production control is a critical element in the operation of an organization in that it controls the major expenditure of resources.

The object of internal auditing is to assist all members of management in the effective discharge of their responsibilities by furnishing them with analyses, appraisals, recommendations, and pertinent comments concerning the activities reviewed. Internal auditors should be concerned with any phase of business activity where they can be of service to management.

Since production control is a critical element in controlling the expenditure of resources, internal auditors should be involved in audits of this function.

AN OVERVIEW OF PRODUCTION CONTROL

Production control exists, either as a formal or informal function, because the objectives of production — to produce the required quantity and quality of goods at the required place and time at an acceptable cost — must be implemented with a view toward the well-being of the company as a whole rather than of the Production Department alone. Having the overall company perspective is important in order to minimize or resolve conflicts in implementing these objectives at the departmental level. Production managers, for example, prefer longer, more economical production runs in order to minimize setup costs. Finance managers prefer shorter runs in order to minimize inventory. Marketing managers prefer a greater inventory of diversified products.

Production control serves as an interface between production and other functions such as engineering, finance, marketing, personnel, and purchasing to provide the necessary planning, coordination and

1

control for effective and efficient production operations relative to the general company objectives.

Production control has always been an important function. In many firms, especially small ones, it exists as an informal system wherein the production personnel interact directly with other departments to produce a coordinated effort. There is a continual expansion and diversification of firms into multiproduct and multiplant operations that increase the complexity of coordinating production with the other operations of the firm. This often results in the creation of production control departments and formal systems.

THE NEED FOR AUDITS OF PRODUCTION CONTROL

Production control is, to a degree, unlike other functions of a business because it is a planning, controlling, and interface function. It is generally a staff rather than a line function. The fact that it is different, however, does not diminish the need to measure and evaluate its effectiveness and efficiency. In light of their experience, training, and professional perspective, internal auditors are in an ideal position to perform these services.

The need for an audit exists whether the production control function is formally or informally defined. If it is an informal system, the effectiveness and efficiency of the system should be measured and evaluated to determine whether a more formal system should be implemented. If it is a formal system, it must be continuously appraised to determine if it works and whether the system adapts sufficiently to the changing requirements of its business environment.

Internal auditing of production control is also a challenge, for it is an area in which internal auditors are not as involved as they are in more traditional areas such as inventory audits. The degree of future involvement must be determined by each internal auditor relative to the needs of the company. It is an area, however, wherein the internal auditor can display initiative as well as respond to a need.

In this monograph, we attempt to provide a comprehensive basis for developing production control audit programs specifically tailored to the needs of individual firms.

RESEARCH METHODOLOGY

The purpose underlying this research project is to describe internal auditors' present role in production control and their anticipated future role. To accomplish this purpose, the basic research consisted of reviewing relevant production control and internal auditing literature, field trips, and a mail questionnaire. This basic research provided a broad perspective.

The more pertinent literature is listed in the bibliography. Nine firms were visited. These represent a cross section of major industries, including the manufacturing of office equipment, construction equipment, heavy factory machinery, automotives, pharmaceuticals, and consumer products as well as a national public accounting firm. The firms were selected because they were involved in internal audits of production control.

The firms visited provided copies of their programs for operational audits of production control and of their audit reports on various situations encountered in these audits. In addition, the firms arranged for in-depth interviews of key personnel in internal auditing, production control, inventory managements, quality control, and production. The documents and interview comments obtained in these visits were the major input for the discussions and audit programs included in this study.

Questionnaires were mailed to 300 members of The Institute of Internal Auditors. The recipients worked for a diversity of manufacturing firms located in numerous countries. We made this selection on the basis that they worked for firms with significant production activity and were officers at either the national or chapter level. The selection criteria were designed to direct the questionnaire toward those who were most likely to have some association with a formal production control function and toward those who would be likely to answer the questionnaire.

Therefore, the sample was not selected on a random basis. Of the 300 questionnaires mailed, 95 (32%) were returned of which 82 (27%) were completed. The questionnaire, a narrative summary of the results, and a numerical summary of the responses are contained in Appendix A.

PLAN OF THE REPORT

Three basic sources — the literature, the field trips, and the questionnaire — provided the information used in the analyses of production control, audit programs, and audit procedures that are reflected herein.

Chapter 2 discusses, in general terms, the role of internal auditors in the area of production control. An overview of the production control function is also included.

Chapter 3 provides detailed audit programs that can be used by internal auditors as a guide in designing and conducting audits of production control.

Chapter 4 discusses practical considerations which internal auditors should take into account when preparing for future audits of production control.

Appendix A presents the results of the questionnaire. Broad descriptions of the physical flow, the information flow, and the interfaces are discussed further in Appendix B for those who might desire a more conceptual and more detailed analysis of production control.

2 ROLE OF THE INTERNAL AUDITOR IN PRODUCTION CONTROL

Modern production systems have become increasingly complex and often involve the manufacture of many products in multiplant locations. Each individual product requires planning and control for obtaining and using the factors of production: machines, manpower, and materials. As product lines expand and as the number of plants increases, planning and control requirements become more critical. More planning and control are needed because production systems must provide a desirable balance between three basic but often conflicting objectives: to provide a maximum quality service to the customer, to provide the most efficient manufacturing operations, and to minimize the investment in inventory.

Even when there is relative stability of consumer demand, of lead time for receiving raw materials from vendors, of machine downtime for repairs, and of other environmental factors, planning and control of production processes is a highly complex effort.

However, production control does not exist in a relatively stable environment. In fact, the principal challenges facing production control personnel relate to the uncertainties involved in predicting the numerous interdependent environmental variables.

Even in a relatively simple, single-product, single-step manufacturing situation, the presence of volatility in just one variable — for example, consumer demand — can make production planning and control more difficult and challenging. In the complex manufacturing processes that characterize most firms today, coordinating production is fraught with a multitude of interdependent, continuously changing variables. As previously noted, many firms have created a formal production control function to provide this coordination. The increasing importance of the production control function, in turn, has necessitated additional involvement by internal auditors. Internal auditors, like production control personnel, must be concerned largely with the dynamics of the environment in which the system operates.

This chapter focuses on the role of the internal auditor in production control. In addition, in order to facilitate this focus, we briefly describe the basic physical flow in the production process, the information flow that is necessary to plan and control the physical flow, and the interfaces among the production control functions and the other functions of the firm.

PRODUCTION PLANNING AND SCHEDULING PROCESS

A simplified overview of the production planning and scheduling process for a single product is shown in Figure 2.1. The process starts with the forecast of consumer demand for the product. This entails an estimate of the quantity demanded at different prices and different levels of advertising and marketing effort.

However, before a specific marketing plan is selected, an estimate must also be made of the total quantity that could be available for sale through a combination of production and allowable reduction of inventory. This analysis of consumer demand, inventory policy, and production capacity is an iterative process that is necessary to equate sales demand with the ability of the firm to provide sufficient goods. Once agreement is reached, the firm can develop a master plan of the level of production required.

Once this master production plan is developed, the bill of materials is utilized to compute the requirements for materials, manpower, and machines. This requirements-planning process forms the basis for purchasing materials and adjusting the reservoirs of manpower and machine facilities, if necessary. Then, on a more detailed basis (e.g., daily or weekly instead of monthly or quarterly), a schedule of production based on the estimated future availability of machine capacity, materials, and manpower is developed to meet the anticipated sales demand which would not be satisfied from inventory adjustments.

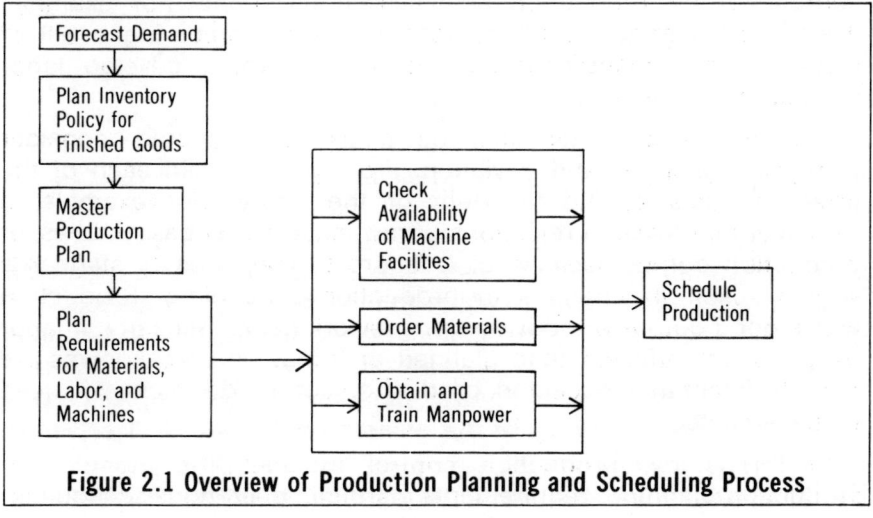

Figure 2.1 Overview of Production Planning and Scheduling Process

ORGANIZATIONAL ASSIGNMENT OF
PRODUCTION CONTROL FUNCTIONS

An overview of the manner in which a typical production organization may divide the various functions of production control is shown in Figure 2.2. Preparing a master production plan (production planning) requires inputs about forecasted demand, actual customer orders, product design engineering standards, and inventory. The master production plan, in turn, is used along with manufacturing engineering and inventory information in planning the requirements for materials, labor, and machines. Once the purchased materials and the planned labor and machine capacities are available, production operations can be scheduled and authorized.

The operation of a complex manufacturing system requires the coordination of many subsystems or modules. Figure 2.3 illustrates the major operations within each of these key production system modules and the interrelationships between these modules. Each key system module encompasses the tasks shown within the smaller boxes. Production planning and control in the broadest sense encompasses all the modules shown. However, in practice, production control usually is defined in a more narrow sense.

Generally, the firms contacted during this study included in production control only the modules of production planning, requirements planning, material and component availability, capacity planning and loading, operations scheduling, and certain aspects of inventory control. In addition, some firms included the purchasing function within the domain of production control.

Although the other modules are not included directly within the production control function by many firms, the production control function must interrelate with these modules in order to plan and coordinate the production activities of the firms. For example, design engineering would be responsible for preparing a bill of materials; and manufacturing engineering would develop labor standards and balance production lines.

Planning and scheduling decisions also should consider significant changes and deviations from plans within each of the three modules at the far right of the figure. For example, a significant increase in rejections of raw materials, subassemblies, or production output because of a failure to meet quality standards should result in changes in production scheduling. Production wants good output without scrap or rework items. Similarly, if labor usage is less efficient than planned or if machine breakdowns are more frequent than expected, production control decisions will need to be adjusted.

In this study, production control includes the modules of production planning, requirements planning, operations scheduling,

6

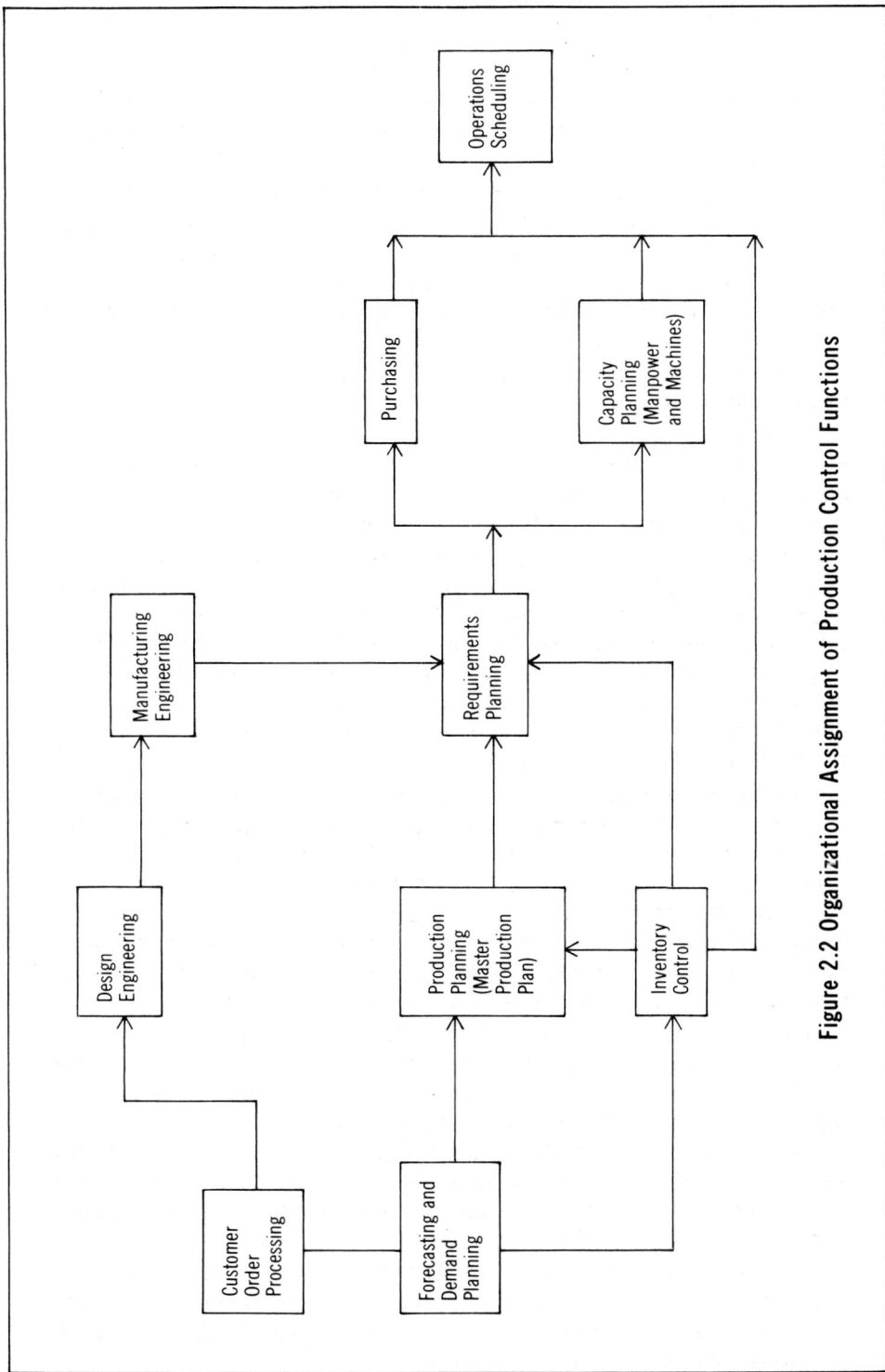

Figure 2.2 Organizational Assignment of Production Control Functions

7

capacity planning and loading, and material component availability with certain inventory control considerations. In addition, audit programs developed in this monograph will focus on the coordination requirements provided by production control with those modules not included directly within the organization unit of production control.

The first step in a broad view of production control occurs in the forecasting and demand-planning system module. Here, the sales demand forecast is developed, based on historical trends, predictions from sales and marketing personnel in the field, and information about current customer orders. The forecast is used to develop a marketing or demand plan which, in turn, is used as input for the finished-goods inventory control plan and the master production plan.

Effective production control requires processing customers' orders properly. When customers' orders are received, they are checked and priced by referring to authorized customer price quotations. If the order is for a product for which no bill of materials has previously been developed, the order is routed to the design engineering module where a standardized or custom bill of materials is prepared. This requires an analysis of the requirements of labor unions and various regulatory bodies as well as analyses of various required engineering changes and their effectiveness. If the customer order is for a standard product, the final goods inventory and the standard bill of materials are checked before the master production plan is modified.

Developing a master schedule for production requires availability checks of key machines, facilities, and components. In the requirements planning module, the bill of materials is used to separate the master schedule into a listing of the gross requirements for materials and components. Information on the availability of components is used to calculate net materials requirements and to develop an ordering plan. This is used for purchasing needed materials and for scheduling production operations.

Operation scheduling requires information about labor requirements from the manufacturing engineering module and about the availability capacities of machine and equipment from the capacity planning and loading module in addition to this information about the availability of materials and components. If all ingredients are available, production control can authorize the start of production and proceed to report the status of the order relative to its location and stage of completion.

A crucial part of production control involves follow-up and expediting orders for critical materials. In this respect, a careful analysis of vendor performance relative to lead time and quality provides valuable planning information.

Finally, feedback on efficiency variances for labor and machine usage provides information for potential adjustment of future labor and machine standards — a type of adaptive control involving product design and manufacturing engineering.

INTERNAL AUDITS OF PRODUCTION CONTROL

The purpose of auditing production control is to ascertain the degree to which production control is fulfilling its role of planning and controlling production to meet the company's objectives of good customer service, efficient plant operations, and low inventory investment. In addition, the purpose of this audit includes recommendations for needed changes in internal controls and operations.

The focus of this audit, as in many audits, should be primarily on internal controls: organization structure, policies and procedures, standards of performance, and records and reports. Before these internal controls are considered, however, the internal auditor should become familiar with the objectives and the operations of production control. This will allow for placing greater emphasis on particular areas and on possible problems within them.

Organization Structure

The audit should appraise the organization structure of production control to evaluate whether the established structure is clearly defined as to duties and responsibilities, whether it contains minimum overlap of responsibilities, and whether the established structure is utilized in the actual operation.

The organization structure should be adequate and comprehensive. It should consider the requirements of production control in the modules of production planning, requirements planning, operations scheduling, capacity planning and loading, material and component availability, and inventory control (see Figure 2.3).

It should also identify and delineate the coordination responsibilities of production control with such areas as demand forecasting, customer order processing, design and manufacturing engineering, purchasing, personnel, quality control, manufacturing cost, and performance reporting and maintenance.

In particular, the organization structure should provide clear communication networks within production control as well as functional areas external to it.

Policies and Procedures

Internal auditors should become familiar with established policies and procedures, verify that they are being adhered to, evaluate whether they provide adequate control, and report their findings.

Policies and procedures should be established to provide that:

■ The master production plan demonstrates the effectiveness of the production control function in resolving conflicts between manufacturing, sales, and financial management relative to the appropriate balance of sales objectives with production and inventory objectives.

■ The master production plan provides an accurate and reliable basis for the master production schedule.

■ The master production schedule reflects the availability of crucial plant and machine capacity and of major components at the time they are needed and at the proper location in multiplant operations.

■ Engineering drawings and specifications are properly and promptly converted into bills of material, production routings, labor standards, and other relevant manufacturing process data that are available for use throughout the firm; and that engineering changes are promptly recognized and implemented.

■ The master production schedule is exploded to provide the gross requirements for manpower, materials, and machines based on the bills of material and the availability of resources.

■ The production order specifies the quantity, quality, and type of goods to be produced and the beginning and completion dates for the order.

■ The production orders are planned and executed:

a. to provide the right quality and quantity of materials at the proper time and place, taking into consideration lead time and the need to minimize inventory investment

b. to consider lead time necessary in order that machine and manpower capacities are balanced to requirements

c. to utilize manpower efficiently and effectively, thus avoiding peak and slack periods and minimizing overtime

d. to utilize machinery efficiently and effectively in order to minimize idle time

e. to provide feedback on the progress of orders

■ Production priorities are appropriately established.

■ Expediting is performed on an organized and timely basis when processing orders.

Standards of Performance

In evaluating the effectiveness of internal controls and of operations, the internal auditor should utilize well-defined, objective standards of performance. These standards of performance provide benchmarks against which to judge such items as lead time, processing time, spoilage, and cost accumulations. Such standards can be identified or developed through discussions with management and through references to industry trends, practices, and statistics.

Records and Reports

Finally, in conducting the audit of production control, the internal auditor should be familiar with the information flows as well as the physical flows. These flows are contained largely in records and reports. The internal auditor must also be concerned with undocumented information flows that comprise the informal system.

Records and reports in all phases of production control should be evaluated as to their timeliness, reliability, and accuracy. In addition, each report should be appraised as to its use and necessity. The internal auditor should evaluate whether records and reports are reliable and accurate descriptions of actual operations and whether they effectively communicate the authorization for manufacturing activities, the results of past operations, and the need for modifications. Records and reports are essential planning and control tools and, as such, are the essence of production control.

ADHERENCE CONTROL AND ADAPTIVE CONTROL

In a relatively stable environment, the internal auditor is concerned largely with the internal controls that are designed to ensure that the planning and control of production conform to the original plans. A system that attempts to make operations conform to the original plan may be referred to as an *adherence control system.*

In a more dynamic environment, the internal auditor must also be concerned with the internal controls that are designed to ensure that production is planned and controlled to adapt to changes in the environment. A system that attempts to effectively adapt production operations to changes may be referred to as an *adaptive control system.*

It should be recognized that no production control system functions in a completely stable or completely dynamic environment. Thus, each production control system must operate as both an adherence control system and as an adaptive control system. In the following discussion, however, the adaptive and adherence aspects of the system are separated for comparison purposes.

Differences Between Adaptive and Adherence Control

The major differences between adaptive and adherence production control systems are identified in Figure 2.4. Although most production control systems involve a blend of both adherence and adaptive systems, a look at these distinctions provides a basis for exploring the essential difference between the two auditing approaches.

The first major difference between adherence and adaptive production control systems is concerned with the emphasis in the information base for the system. In a relatively stable environment, future events and relationships are predictable largely on the basis of statistical analyses of historical data. When the environment is stable, these historically based predictions should be sufficiently accurate and reliable to become the nucleus for the planning and control system. Of course, even in a relatively stable environment, production systems will still be changed. Consequently, the historical data base is supplemented by management's estimates of future changes and by certain current information.

Dimension	Type of System	
	Adherence System	Adaptive System
1. Information Base	Historical Data (supplemented by managerial discretion and some current data; e.g., customer sales orders)	Current Data (supplemented by managerial discretion and historical data)
2. Starting Point for Planning and Coordination Actions	Predictable, starting point is sales forecasts or customer orders	Unpredictable, starting point is a change in any relevant production control variable
3. Frequency	Periodic forecasting with some updating when customer orders are processed	Continuous monitoring of all relevant production control variables
4. Lead Time Before Decision Output Is Required	Long — for reactions to forecasts Intermediate — for reactions to customer orders	Short

Figure 2.4 Differences Between Adaptive and Adherence Systems

Not all current information, however, is pertinent. For example, an adherence control system normally processes information about new customer orders; but it is not expected to detect and process information signals about changes such as (1) the differences between expected and actual lead time for materials, (2) the temporary changes in routing patterns and machine usage initiated on the production line, and (3) postponements of the required dates for some materials (unexpediting) because other materials needed to produce the item were discovered to be unavailable until a later time.

The second difference is related to the starting point for the process of planning and coordinating the production system responses to information. The adherence system has predictable starting points. For developing the annual master production plan, the starting point is the sales forecast. For developing specific production release orders, the starting point is the customer order. In an adaptive control system, the starting point is unpredictable. It occurs at any point when a change in a relevant production control variable is detected. Changes that trigger adaptive control reactions may occur in any module contained in Figure 2.3.

Third, the frequency of control actions differs between the two systems. In an adherence system, control actions occur when a forecast is made and when a customer order is received. In an adaptive control system, monitoring all relevant production control variables for signals of changes should occur on a continuous basis.

The fourth difference is concerned with the amount of lead time available between receiving information and the point when control actions — usually in the form of decision outputs — are required. In the adherence system, the lead time required to react to periodic sales forecasts is relatively long. For example, many firms begin developing their annual sales forecasts and annual production plans two or three months prior to the beginning of the current year. The lead time allowable to react to customer orders is shorter (e.g., two weeks to three months for many firms) but not as short as the lead time allowable for most adaptive control decisions. For example, when a machine breaks down or a vendor communicates a delay in supplying critical material, the adaptive control system must immediately reassess its production priorities and issue revised production schedules.

An effective production control system will accommodate the essential aspects of both adherence and adaptive control. Many firms have production control systems that are adequate when the environment is stable; however, these systems are unsatisfactory because they fail to react quickly and reliably to the changes encountered in a dynamic environment. Thus, it is desirable for the internal auditor to test both aspects of the system.

Implications for the Internal Auditor

We have found that the function of production control is receiving increased attention on the part of internal auditors. To date, however, few guidelines have been written for internal audits of production control. In addition, what has been written concentrates primarily on *formal systems* which attempt to control operations in order to adhere to *original plans* for sales, production, materials, labor, machine utilization, and inventories. These systems are referred to as *adherence control systems.*

On the other hand, little has been written about internal audits designed to test whether the production control system responds quickly, accurately, and reliably to environmental changes such as revisions in customer due dates, unanticipated machine break-downs, absences in key labor personnel, or unusual lead times for raw materials ordered from vendors. If such environmental changes occur, attempts to adhere to the original plans could actually be harmful. Instead, production control should change (adapt) the production plan to reflect the new environmental conditions.

Accordingly, when a firm operates in a rapidly changing environment — as is typical under today's economic conditions — internal auditors should place much greater emphasis on testing *adaptive control* rather than relying only upon tests of adherence to original plans. To determine the effectiveness of adaptive control, internal auditors should test both the formal and informal organizational communication systems. It is the adaptiveness of the formal control system that is the most important issue. The test of the informal system is designed primarily to determine under what conditions the adaptiveness of the formal system is inadequate. Once this is known, necessary modifications of the formal system may be made.

A Major Audit Problem — Lack of Evidence of Relevant Changes in the Formal System

One of the greatest difficulties with audits of an adaptive control system is the lack of source documents that detail changes in relevant variables. In an adherence system, the internal auditor can find source documentation in the form of sales forecasts and custom orders. Such source documents provide a reliable, objective starting point for audit verification. For example, the internal auditor can start with a sample of customer orders and retrace the flow of information through production schedules, bills of materials, inventory checks, purchasing orders, receiving reports, capacity loadings, authorized production releases, status reports, and production performance reports (see Figure 2.3). This process provides evidence as to whether all customer orders are appropriately reflected in the final production reports, but it will not detect an item on the final report that is not supported by a customer order or other appropriate source document.

The internal auditors could then check to see whether all items on the final report are supported by customer orders or other appropriate source documents by reversing the previous process. Thus, they may start by selecting a sample of final production reports and vouching these reports to the original source documents. Such "dual-direction" sampling procedures provide a comprehensive audit. Unfortunately, this approach is more difficult in testing the effectiveness of adaptive controls because of the lack of original source documents indicating the need for adaptive control action.

There are two basic reasons for the lack of documentation of changes that trigger adaptive control action. First, many firms rely upon the informal system to detect such changes and to provide corrective action through an informal network that operates outside the formal system. In these cases, the firm does not expect the formal system to be completely accurate nor to be a guide for adaptive production control action. Thus, if a firm uses the informal system to communicate adaptive control information, the internal auditor must necessarily look outside the formal information system for cues indicating that relevant changes have occurred. Unfortunately, as discussed more extensively in Appendix B, there are limitations and disadvantages with informal systems.

The second reason for the lack of documentation of relevant changes is that many firms attempting to use the formal system for adaptive control either fail to continuously monitor the relevant production control variables for significant changes or fail to properly enter documentation of such changes into the formal system. The audit implication is the same as when an informal system is used — the internal auditor must search outside the formal production control system for evidence about such changes.

ADAPTIVE CONTROL AUDIT PROCEDURES

Audit tests of adaptive control are necessarily quite different from tests of adherence control. Tests of adherence control center upon verifying that a proper response was made to items which have *already entered the formal information system.* However, tests of adaptive control focus upon responses to environmental changes, even though such changes are often never recorded in the formal information system. The cue for adaptive control often lies *outside* the information system, whereas the cue for adherence control generally lies *inside* the system. Therefore, in audits of adaptive control much greater emphasis must be placed upon gathering evidence from the informal information system, primarily through interviews with key personnel. Thus, audit interviews can provide the auditor with a basis for an analysis of the formal production control system and its ability to respond to environmental changes.

In many cases, the internal auditor can gather probablistic evidence related to adaptive control. For example, falsely stating an earlier-than-necessary due date may have — but need not have — one of two results. First, the goods may be produced in accordance with the recorded due date but allowed to sit around before shipment. On the other hand, the goods may be completed and shipped in accordance with the recorded due date; but the customer may justify delayed payment by stating that the goods were received before they were actually needed. Both of these results — delay in shipping and delay in customer payment — produce some evidential matter. Unfortunately, such evidential matter is not always conclusive. The presence of evidence of delays in shipping or collecting receivables does not necessarily mean that marketing personnel stated an earlier-than-needed due date. Likewise, the absence of such evidence does not necessarily mean that due dates are accurately stated.

Such lack of certainty of this audit evidence does not render it useless. Rather, its probablistic nature points to a significant difference between evidential matter for adaptive and adherence control. For adherence control, primary audit evidence comes from the formal system and is supplemented by evidence from the informal system. Conversely, for adaptive control, primary audit evidence comes from the informal system and is supplemented by evidence from the formal system. Both types of audits may use the same techniques, but the emphasis is different.

Status of Production Order Completion	Status of Customer Delivery	Possible Problem Areas
Late	Late	Total lead time inadequate Production problems Material shortages Scheduling problems
Late	Early	Total lead time excessive Manufacturing lead time inadequate Production problems Material shortages Scheduling problems
Early	Late	Manufacturing lead time excessive Total lead time inadequate Warehousing or shipping problems
Early	Early	Total lead time excessive Manufacturing lead time excessive Excessive inventory available Improper scheduling Favored handling of customers Inadequate standards Changing of production priorities

**Figure 2.5 Status of Completion and Delivery Dates —
Signals of Production Control Problems**

Throughout the examination, the internal auditor should be alert to the basic signs of potential problems. The two areas wherein signs of production control problems most frequently appear concern (1) the status of production order completion dates and (2) the status of customer delivery dates. If the firm is characteristically late or if it is excessively early in completion or delivery of goods, the internal auditor should be alert for the associated production control problems. Figure 2.5 shows the relationship between the status of these items and possible production control problems that could cause the condition. These possible relationships should guide the auditor in gathering and analyzing evidence about the adaptiveness of production control.

ADAPTIVE CONTROL AUDIT OBJECTIVES

The basic objective of auditing production control adaptiveness is to obtain sufficient, reliable evidence that all significant changes in relevant production control variables were quickly and accurately detected and that proper, timely adjustments to these changes were made in the production control system.

The audit procedures should adequately test whether the system properly adapts to changes in:

- Sales forecasts
- Required delivery dates for customer orders
- Priorities for product availability
- Types or quantities of required materials
- Appropriate inventory models
- Expected lead time for materials to be ordered
- Expected dates for receiving materials already on order
- Expediting priorities or procedures
- Available inventory and required production time for subassembly and component parts
- Types and quantities of required labor
- Composition of the labor force and the availability of different types of labor
- Types and quantitites of machine requirements and capacities
- Warehousing requirements and availabilities
- Shipping requirements and availabilities

This chapter discusses the role of the internal auditor in production control in general terms. More detailed descriptions of the modules contained in Figure 2.3 and the audit programs that are applicable to these modules are presented in the following chapter.

3 INTERNAL AUDIT PROGRAM FOR PRODUCTION CONTROL

This chapter provides a detailed audit program which may be used as a guide for internal auditors in designing and conducting audits of production control. The major components of production control are also discussed in greater detail and their direct relation to the internal audit program is explained.

This chapter focuses on a modular approach to the internal audit of the production control function. Audit objectives and procedures are described relative to each specific phase or operation of the production control function presented in Figure 2.3. This modular approach was recommended strongly by firms that were interviewed during the field study portion of the project, largely on the basis that it provided greater flexibility. A complete audit of the production control function was seldom undertaken by these firms because of time and manpower constraints.

In addition, certain modules needed less attention by the internal auditor. This was particularly true of those modules that existed in a relatively stable environment. For example, the interface of design engineering and manufacturing engineering with manufacturing operations required less attention than production planning or operation scheduling.

However, it should be stressed that, even though internal auditors' attention is normally directed toward a particular phase of production control, they should always consider the inter-relationship of the segment under audit with other phases of production control and, in fact, with other functions of the entire business operation.

A separate audit program is presented for each module of the production planning and control system shown in Figure 2.3. However, in order to provide a more integrated discussion, the 14 modules are grouped into four general categories: sales forecasting, production planning, inventory control, and production scheduling.

GENERAL REVIEW

For internal auditors to properly evaluate the production control function, they need a thorough understanding of the organization structure, production facilities, nature of products and market conditions, production system, and information system being used. Therefore, a general review of these factors is the proper starting point for the internal audit.

Understanding the organization structure normally necessitates obtaining or preparing an organization chart, identifying work responsibilities and reporting relationships, and obtaining job descriptions for key personnel. A tour of the manufacturing facilities will allow the observation of basic production processes, physical flows of materials, machine arrangements, and interactions between personnel and equipment. Auditors should observe the operation of the information processing system to identify major sources of information about production orders, schedules, authorizations, inventory levels, and manufacturing performance. A review of the firm's financial information will often provide guidance in areas where it is most likely that operations are out of control or the information flow is unreliable, misleading, or inadequate for decision making. Some information cues which may be used to appropriately direct auditors' attention concern are:

- Inventory turnover rates
- The percentage of total production costs attributable to direct materials and to labor
- Recent product line trends
- Gross margin and profits by product line
- Seasonal sales and production patterns
- Analysis of returns and allowances
- Standard cost variances

These considerations and many more are included in the general review of the audit program which follows.

Audit Program: General Review

1. Obtain and review a copy of the organization chart for the department. (Are the assignments of responsibility clear and reasonable for effective internal control?)

2. Ascertain that the individual in charge of Production Control reports to an executive whose organizational level assures top-management support.

3. Check on the existence of a Production Control policy manual or other written instructions and review for adequacy.

4. Obtain and appraise the adequacy of all statements of mission, organizational purpose, and major policy relating to the department.

5. Describe the missions of the different departments and agencies involved with Production Control, spelling out any divided responsibilities and the basis of the division.

   Determine that responsibilities are assigned in a reasonable manner to eliminate erroneous splits which could lead to duplications of effort and the creation of production schedules which are not responsive to manufacturing requirements.

   Determine whether the number of agencies involved in these functions is excessive to the point where effective feedback of information is jeopardized.

6. Establish whether written procedures exist for the internal guidance of Production Control personnel and for the coordination of production activities.

7. If the department is decentralized on a line basis, review and appraise the manner in which responsibilities are assigned and coordinated.

8. Review and appraise the adequacy of job descriptions.

9. Ascertain whether Production Control has an effective voice with Sales and Manufacturing regarding the efficient balance of production and inventory costs with customer requirements. (Also, determine if production is "make to order" or "make to stock.")

10. What procedures exist for maintaining liaison with the following groups:

    Purchasing — for orders placed and late delivery by vendors?

    Quality Control — for expediting material through Incoming Inspection?

    Engineering — for coordination of engineering change orders?

11. Review procedures to determine that they cover:

    ■ Finished product inventory forecasting and planning techniques
    ■ Manner of receiving production requirements
    ■ How input needs are transmitted to other company groups who will procure such inputs
    ■ Internal planning criteria

- Receival of inputs
- Control of processing operations
- Relations with support activities
- Relations with quality control, especially as to jurisdictional control
- Internal production records
- Inventory-taking requirements
- Union relations
- Component parts forecasting and planning techniques
- Inventory record keeping
- Requisitioning of raw materials
- Stores administration of all classes of inventories
- Routing, scheduling, and dispatching
- Production reporting
- Labor control, including timekeeping, reporting, and measuring labor efficiency
- Coordination with the product design and industrial engineering
- Other miscellaneous functions

12. What procedures are followed to ensure that the Production Control manual is always up-to-date?

13. Ascertain the extent to which the system is: (a) Manual, (b) Mechanized, (c) Computerized.

14. Obtain manpower data for the Production Control Department as follows:

	Number
Production Control managers	_____
Production Control supervisors	_____
Schedulers	_____
Clerks	_____
Expediters	_____

15. What method is used to standardize routing paperwork operations within the entire Production Control operation?

16. Is there in effect a work order or similar system that requires written orders for all major production jobs?

17. If *yes* and if shop work order numbers are used, can they be eliminated by identifying parts by number on the schedule?

18. Obtain work load statistics for the Production Control Department as follows:

	Number Annually	Per Day Per Production Employee
Sales orders	_____	_____
Production orders	_____	_____
Sales order changes	_____	_____
Manufacturing process sheets	_____	_____
Bills of material (if separate from manufacturing process sheet)	_____	_____
Purchase requisitions	_____	_____
Material withdrawal requisitions	_____	_____
Other forms	_____	_____

19. Evaluate the adequacy of the number and types of personnel by referring to the data above and by analyzing overtime statistics for the period under review.

   Determine the reasons for excessive amounts of overtime by discussion with appropriate supervision.

   By reference to personnel statistics, determine whether turnover of personnel appears excessive and obtain reasons therefor.

20. Obtain an ABC classification of inventories divided into raw materials, purchased parts, manufactured parts, and finished goods (Determine whether procedures are specified properly for each category.).

21. Ascertain the extent to which the system is based on:

   ■ Order-point techniques
   ■ Requirements planning
   ■ Dependent or independent demand

22. Describe the nature of production. Is it:

   ■ Single process?
   ■ Multiple process?
   ■ Single product?
   ■ Multiple product?
   ■ Raw material and/or purchased parts to semifinished or finished product?
   ■ Other?

23. Prepare statistics for the past two years (current and prior years) showing:

    Sales

    Cost of sales broken down into components, direct and indirect materials, direct and indirect labor, direct and indirect overhead

24. Has there been any significant problem this year in meeting delivery schedules? If so, what were the circumstances and the solutions proposed or adopted?

25. How many delivery schedules were missed last month? last year? three years ago? How many of these were missed for the second time? the third time? and so on?

26. If there is a month-end overloading problem in manufacturing, what share does Production Control contribute to this problem?

27. To what extent are there significant accumulations of incomplete assemblies or subassemblies being held up in process because of:

    ■ Shortages of parts?
    ■ Starting work ahead of schedule or without reference to the schedules?
    ■ Work being held up for inspection?
    ■ Work being held up for repairs and/or replacement of defective components?
    ■ Work being held up because of equipment or manpower overloads at the next station?
    ■ Lack of proper identification and/or routing?

28. What has been the trend over the past three fiscal years in the ratio of purchased components to manufactured components?

29. What types of comparative cost data are available to assist in the make-or-buy decisions?

30. What amount of subcontracting was done over the past year?

31. Are make-or-buy decisions reviewed so that proper consideration is given to purchasing, production, and engineering viewpoints?

32. If *yes*, is the review process structured so that make-or-buy decisions are quickly made?

33. Is plant production per employee, per dollar of wages, and per dollar of plant investment known?

34. If *yes*, do the figures show that plant efficiency has kept pace with or risen faster than that of others in the industry?

35. If *no*, are steps being taken to improve efficiency?

36. By examining a representative number of production orders, determine whether production practices reflect rush or emergency conditions.

Indicate the incidence and nature of these conditions in the work papers and their relationship to the total production orders tested.

Determine whether such conditions merely reflect special handling of orders of favored customers and items generally considered critical or whether they represent genuine emergencies which may lead to breaking existing setups, incurring overtime by production personnel, or inducing waivers of quality standards.

SALES FORECASTS AND ORDER PROCESSING

The discussion in this section includes modules A and B of Figure 2.3: sales forecasting and customer order processing. Although sales forecasting is initially the responsibility of the marketing function, it is included in the internal audit program for production control because it is the beginning point for production planning and provides crucial information for both production scheduling and inventory control. Production control personnel usually participate in planning total business volume and determining the product line details of the forecast. Long-run sales forecasts provide the basis for planning production facilities. Short-run sales forecasts are the basis for the production plan which, in turn, is used for labor-force planning and inventory planning control.

The audit program for sales forecasting includes a review of forecasting procedures, responsibilities, and time schedules with special attention given to the interface between the annual profit plan and long-range and short-range sales forecasts. A comparison of recent forecasts with actual demand is useful in evaluating forecasting accuracy.

Reviewing forecasting procedures should determine the degree of reliance upon external forecasts of national and international economic conditions, industrial trends, technological developments, and market mechanisms. Statistical forecasting procedures and underlying assumptions should be ascertained and evaluated. In addition, internal auditors should gather and evaluate information used in revising the detailed sales forecasts, giving attention to whether lead times are adequate.

Internal audits of the customer order processing module are designed to test whether procedures are established and consistently followed to assure that customer orders are properly prepared, reviewed, and communicated to production planning personnel on a timely basis. Internal auditors should verify that delivery dates specified to customers give proper consideration to production and inventory constraints, are reasonably attainable, and reflect customer needs realistically.

An effective system of planning production priorities may be sabotaged by sales personnel listing earlier-than-necessary delivery dates. This usually results in expediting orders which could be delayed without problems and delaying critically needed orders.

An effective audit program, therefore, will include procedures to test whether the formal due dates are accurate and reliable and whether changes in promised delivery dates are quickly and effectively communicated.

These factors and many others are included in the following audit programs for sales forecasting and customer order processing:

Audit Program: Sales Forecasts

1. Are sales forecasts communicated to production so that schedules can be developed to authorize production to best meet customer requirements, order patterns, and inventory requirements?

2. Verify that sales forecasts are prepared.

3. Is sufficient documentary support for the sales forecasts provided?

4. Are changes likely to affect significantly the forecasted sales of products communicated quickly to production in writing?

5. Verify the procedures for translating sales forecasts to production plans.

6. Are sales forecasts prepared in the detail needed for ready translation into a specific production plan? (If *yes*, secure a copy of such a forecast and append it to the working papers.)

7. Where forecasts are used to plan inventory levels, verify that they include sufficient factual data for each product or product line.

8. Compare the predicted and actual sales order for each major product category for each month (Make inquiries about variances).

Audit Program: Customer Order Processing

1. Test a representative number of customer orders to determine the time lag existing between the date the order is received in house to the date received by Production Control.

2. Are the formal due dates accurate and reliable?

3. Review the techniques used when confirming delivery dates to customers to determine if:

   ▪ Delivery dates not confirmed, catalog terms served as an alternative indication.
   ▪ Delivery dates are confirmed by a separate advice.
   ▪ Delivery dates confirmed by day? week? month?

4. Indicate the bases used in establishing delivery dates, outlining approval required, approving department, and method used in making the delivery date calculation.

5. Review the details substantiating a sample of calculated delivery dates and comment on their completeness and adequacy.

6. Do sales (marketing) personnel show an earlier due date than necessary in order to allow for a margin of safety if production is behind schedule?

7. If the formal due dates are artificially set at an earlier-than-necessary date, is the real slack time informally communicated to production control personnel?

8. Are rush orders and expedited orders ever completed and then allowed to sit around before being shipped?

9. Do customers ever delay payment after receiving goods, stating that they did not wish goods delivered so soon?

10. Compare the recorded completion dates with dates of shipment to customers. For any unusual delays, obtain evidence, by inquiry or by confirmation, that the delay in shipping was not because the due date requested by the customer was later than the due date specified on the sales order (or bill of materials).

11. Scan customer correspondence files and any attachments to sales orders for possible evidence of customers' requested delivery dates (Compare the delivery dates requested in such correspondence with the specified due dates listed on the corresponding sales order).

12. Scan attachments to sales invoices for indications of a difference between customer's requested delivery date and the due date on the sales order.

13. Scan any attachments to source documents for cash collections of receivables for indications of a difference between customer's requested delivery date and the due date on the sales order.

14. Ascertain whether late delivery has resulted in, or could result in, fines, loss of business, or exchange losses on foreign trade. Determine what action was taken to avoid its occurrence or recurrence.

15. Determine whether formal lead time schedules are utilized in establishing delivery dates for confirmation to customers.

16. Obtain (or prepare) copies of the most recent lead time schedules for major products and ascertain the departments involved and times allotted for each.

17. Evaluate the completeness and reasonableness of the lead time schedules (Establish whether an allowance for administrative and clerical processing time is included).

    Select a sample of production orders related to the lead time schedules and, by reference to Production Control records, calculate the actual time expended in the manufacturing process for these parts and compare this to the established lead time schedule.

    Discuss variances with appropriate supervisors where required.

18. By adding lead times to the dates of receipts of a representative sample of customer orders, determine whether delivery can be made as promised.

    Where confirmed delivery dates do not allow sufficient lead time, discuss findings with Production Control supervision to determine whether additional cost may be incurred because of rush procurement, overtime in production, breaks of existing setups, etc., caused by unrealistic delivery dates.

    Where possible, obtain an estimate of cost increases due to providing a shorter-than-required lead time.

    Where an excessively long lead time is provided, determine the control exercised to prevent the buildup of relatively large finished-goods inventories (In this regard, tests should be made of items on hand in the shipping dock or staging area to determine whether they were completed substantially ahead of schedule).

19. Is information as to lengthening lead time due to heavy order volume fed back to the Sales Department so that delivery promises can be adjusted accordingly?

20. Discuss with Production Control supervisors the procedures in effect for plant selection where there is a choice of plant in which an order can be produced (Review and evaluate the bases used in making the determination).

21. Assess the methods employed to determine whether required goods can be produced from stock or whether they must be assembled to order.

22. Ascertain whether, and by whom, promised delivery dates are compared to actual (Summarize the results and indicate what corrective action was taken or is required).

23. Verify that changes in customer orders are recognized on a timely basis; i.e., specifications, quantity, and delivery.

24. Review time required to recognize customer's request.

25. Are customers informed in advance of shipping dates which will probably not be met?

26. Is there a report to management for each change in the promised date to a customer?

27. Establish whether order changes present a problem by examining a representative number of changes to determine the reasons for change (Use the following schedule).

	Number
Customer requested change in delivery schedule	_____
Customer requested change in product specifications	_____
Customer furnished delivery or release date where none had been indicated previously	_____
Change resulting from in-house adjustments (including errors)	_____
Total tested	_____

Ascertain the extent to which each of the categories above contributed to production delays and/or the buildup of excess inventory levels.

Determine what action was initiated to minimize unwarranted changes resulting from in-house adjustments.

28. Review return-goods procedures and age returns not yet accounted for.

29. Verify that returns are authorized and properly accounted for.

PRODUCTION PLANNING

The discussion in this section includes not only the Production Planning module (E) but also those for Design Engineering (C) and Manufacturing Engineering (D). The purpose of production planning is to select the plan of action which will provide the productive capacity desired for the period specified in the demand forecast. Later, when more precise information about specific customer orders is available, productive capacity will be allocated to certain products as a part of the production *scheduling* process. In developing a periodic production plan, top management will usually consider sales forecasts, product costs, machine and labor processing capacities, inventory-holding costs, seasonality factors, subcontracting alternatives, and the feasibility of major modifications in plant, equipment, and work force.

Internal audits of the Production Planning module are designed to verify whether the master production schedule appropriately integrates information about forecasted sales and available capacities for machines, plant, materials, component parts, warehousing, and shipping. Since the master production schedule depends on all this information, the audit must be extended to include tests of the reliability and accuracy of each of these information sources. Production plans may be misleading because of inaccurate or unreliable data sources, because of errors in communicating the information to Production Planning, or because Production Planning fails to properly integrate all the information into a coordinated master plan. Therefore, the auditors must direct their attention to all three potential error points: source, transmittal, and integration. The procedures shown in the audit program for the production planning module are designed to do this.

The audit program for the Design Engineering module specifies procedures which can be used to evaluate whether a currently attainable, accurate, usable, and sufficiently detailed bill of material is prepared for each product. Evidence of significant changes in prices, quantities or qualities of required materials, labor, and machines should be reviewed to determine whether bills of materials are changed appropriately.

Audits of Manufacturing Engineering are designed to evaluate whether appropriate procedures are followed to assure that there is proper sequencing of production operations, routing of parts and materials, and balancing of production lines. The auditors should review the engineering time studies, statistical analyses, and labor-force assumptions used in developing assembly labor standards.

The audit programs for Design Engineering, Manufacturing Engineering, and Production Planning follow.

Audit Program: Design Engineering

1. Is a bill of material including work flows and sequences prepared for each product?

2. When a bill of materials is prepared, is it kept current?

3. Is someone responsible for keeping drawings and bills of materials up-to-date?

4. Are bills of materials or usage formulas that are up-to-date (reflecting the latest engineering changes) the basis for determining parts requirements?

5. For a sample of bills of materials, vouch that the materials, labor, and machine requirements conform with engineering standards.

6. Are there written procedures covering the format and content of engineering paperwork (bills of material, parts list, blueprints, etc.) and its maintenance on a timely basis?

7. Are bills of material (or order lists) computer generated?

8. Does the company have a formal value-analysis program seeking substitution of less costly materials, ways of using the same part, and insuring that qualities of parts do not exceed usage requirements of end products?

9. Are engineering changes adequately controlled through the system?

10. Are all engineering change notices promptly forwarded to Production Control?

11. Are all changes analyzed for effect on excess and obsolescence?

12. Is one individual assigned the responsibility for maintaining an up-to-date record of engineering changes and following up to insure timely incorporation of such changes?

13. Does Production complain about inadequate designs, designs that cannot be fabricated easily, or too frequent design changes?

14. Does Production complain about late deliveries of new designs and design changes that alter production schedules or delay production?

15. What effect do engineering or production change notices have on the month-end overloading problem?

16. Is there a procedure under which the Production Department can get quick approval on requests for temporary deviations from engineering specifications?

17. Determine whether the requirements calculation includes an allowance to cover scrap, shrinkage, and other nonproductive usage (Was the calculation made by Engineering, and when was it last updated?).

18. Is reporting of material usage, scrap, and production by part and operation made available to engineering personnel so that specific material usage and scrap standards can be evaluated?

19. Are the results of quality control, product testing, and evaluation passed on to Engineering?

20. If the production plan is based on a material requirements system, determine that the following are maintained and updated:

    Item master record showing part number description, unit of measure, balance on hand, receipts, issues, setup time, running time, key machine group where item begins processing, family identification, etc.

    Product structure record — the bill of materials which links the components together

21. Ascertain whether special lead time is required in connection with product design changes, special tooling, or similar customarily time-consuming problems.

    Schedule average lead times for these special situations in work papers.

    Determine whether these items might have been overlooked in establishing lead times, thereby building in a late delivery at the inception of the order.

22. Determine if bills of material are complete and if they are available to the shop on a timely basis.

    Ascertain when the bills of material were last reviewed as to their current status.

    Determine the frequency of processing changes to the bills of material and the techniques employed in updating.

    Determine the time lag in processing engineering changes in Production Control by reviewing the dates of selected engineering change notices on hand which are not yet processed by Production Control.

    When the time delay appears excessive, discuss with appropriate supervision and obtain reasons for delays.

    If current production is affected by these engineering changes, determine whether advance copies are forwarded to Manufacturing, Quality Control, and other affected departments to permit them to confirm to the change.

    Trace several of the parts involved with engineering changes to the manufacturing process sheets on the production floor to verify that advance copies were properly routed and posted in emergency situations.

23. Select a sample of recent engineering change notices and verify that they were posted to the bills of material.

    Review the engineering change notices for proper approvals.

Summarize the major reasons for engineering changes noted in the sample selected (e.g., cost reduction, quality improvement, correction, etc.).

24. Review the basis for determining the effective point for implementing an engineering change.

Outline in the work papers the procedures and routines employed in establishing the effective point.

Examine backup documentation used to establish this point and evaluate for completeness, especially noting those cases where all materials available become obsolete as a result of the change.

25. Review the methods in effect to modify, remove, or dispose of parts made obsolete by engineering changes and give consideration to the following as part of the substitution:

- Using the stock of old parts before the new part is bought or fabricated
- Reworking the old part
- Returning the old part to the vendor
- Assuring that obsolete materials are segregated in a controlled stores area

26. Accumulate the value of stock on hand of parts which became obsolete as a result of the engineering change notices sampled.

Number of engineering changes   _____
Dollar value of obsolete parts   _____

Audit Program: Manufacturing Engineering

1. Do all major jobs and operations have time standards established by industrial engineering methods?

2. Is there a continuous program to review and revise methods and standards?

3. Does the Industrial Engineering Department establish standard time data to minimize the amount of time studies that must be made?

4. Is there evidence that Industrial Engineering estimates (standards) are current?

5. Verify that Manufacturing Engineering considers all levels of production critical to the finished output.

6. Review Manufacturing Engineering documents to determine if fabrication, assembly, subassembly, and final assembly are covered.

7. Are changes in labor hours (direct and indirect) per unit of output communicated quickly and accurately?

8. Is reporting of labor utilization and efficiency by operation made available to engineering personnel so that specific labor standards can be evaluated?

9. Are Manufacturing Department people in agreement with the time standards used?

10. Are process or routing sheets available (for all parts) which provide detail as to how each part and assembly is to be made?

11. Are tests on the efficiency of the machines, standard to manufacturer's specifications, periodically conducted?

12. Was there economic justification for the original acquisition of machines? Has it since been tested?

13. Is machinery as technologically modern as is economically feasible? Is there evidence of a current review of machine technology?

14. Appraise the adequacy of analysis and supporting documentation for major plant layout determinations.

15. Obtain standard cost-variance reports for materials, labor, and machine utilization (Scan the explanations of variances for references to obsolete standards which should have been revised).

16. Compare actual with predicted production time for subassemblies and component parts (Inquire as to explanations of variances).

17. Select a number of high usage and high dollar value fabricated or assembled parts appearing in the major bills of material; ascertain that manufacturing process sheets (routing sheets, production process sheets, material travelers) are available for these parts and contain at least the following data:

   ■ Quantity and specifications of material required to make the part
   ■ Sequence of operations
   ■ Preferred department and machine or work center where each operation is performed
   ■ Operator motion sequence
   ■ Standard time allowed for each operation
   ■ Special tools, jigs, or fixtures required
   ■ Accepted tolerance for scrap, breakage, etc.
   ■ Accepted tolerance for downtime during operation

(Review the system used for maintaining these documents on a current basis and comment on its adequacy.)

Audit Program: Production Planning

1. Is a master production schedule used as the basis of planning production?

2. Are written sales forecasts utilized to develop the master production schedule?

3. Verify that the master production schedule is in agreement with sales forecasts or confirmed customer orders as appropriate.

4. Compare units shown on the master production schedule to the forecast or to customer orders as appropriate.

5. Verify that the master production schedule is revised in a timely and efficient manner.

6. If component parts and subassemblies are produced, do their production schedules tie in with end-product schedules?

7. Does Production Planning predict the work load for each machine in sufficient detail to permit early forecasting of manpower and/or machine priority needs?

8. Determine if the production plan is periodically updated to reflect changes in order input, forecasts, and/or other management revisions.

   Note frequency of review and modifications.

   Ascertain that recipients of the original plan also receive copies of modifications.

   Where the plan is modified, evaluate whether unstarted shop orders and major open purchase commitments are reviewed for possible cancellation, reduction, or increase.

9. Determine whether the master production schedule is updated by "regeneration" (i.e., throwing away the previous plan and starting over with a new one) or by "net change" (introducing into the master plan only those changes made since the last plan was issued).

10. Are plant and machine capacities known and documented in sufficient detail to allow accurate planning?

11. Determine that shipping capacities are known and up-to-date.

12. Determine that warehouse space availability is known and up-to-date.

13. Determine whether accurate information is available concerning the feasibility of adjusting plant capacity during the period covered by the master production plan.

14. Verify that adjustments of plant capacity are given appropriate consideration in developing the master production schedule.

15. Obtain a copy of the overall production plan for the year (Ascertain whether the plan was approved).

> Determine the organization responsible for preparation of the plan.

> Ascertain the degree of participation of Production Control in developing the production plan.

> Assess the degree of detail and quality of the content of the plan.

> Establish that the plan is distributed to all appropriate parties.

INVENTORY CONTROL

The discussion in this section includes the modules for Requirements Planning (F), Inventory Control (G), Material and Component Availability (H), and Purchasing (I). Internal audits of the Requirements Planning module test whether procedures are established and implemented to assure that the master production schedule is properly integrated with bills of material to adequately estimate the various materials and components required during the planning period.

The audit should test whether proper consideration has been given to those materials and components which are already on hand, those on open order, and those needed for production orders which have been issued but not yet filled. The audit program also gathers evidence about actual production priorities — as opposed to formally stated priorities — and about the processing of changes in production requirements.

Audits of Inventory Control are designed to determine both the formally prescribed and actually operationalized policies for obtaining needed materials and components. Evidence is gathered to test whether appropriate consideration is given to inventory carrying costs, ordering costs, and out-of-stock costs. For each major material or component, the audit program tests all of the actually implemented procedures for determining *when* and *how much* to order. To accomplish this the internal auditor discovers and documents (1) the methods for classifying inventory by annual dollar value (such as the ABC method), (2) the stewardship and reporting controls for various classes of inventory, and (3) the interrelationships between demand for various types of inventory (i.e., whether demand for an item is independent or dependent). Finally, in order to operationally audit inventory control effectiveness, the auditor must evaluate whether the inventory models in use are appropriate.

The objective of the audit program for the Material and Component Availability module is to gather evidence to evaluate whether there is a proper integration of requirements planning information and inventory availability information. The auditor should identify and evaluate the procedures used by the firm to determine whether major materials and components are available, to coordinate anticipated production usage with anticipated receipts of materials from vendors, and to properly set aside materials which are committed for scheduled production.

The audit program for Purchasing tests whether vendor information is accurate, reliable, and current; whether prompt action is taken on purchase requests; whether accurate information about the status of outstanding purchase orders is maintained; and whether current expediting efforts are effective and consistent with scheduling priorities. To accomplish all this, the internal auditor gathers evidence from vendor files, open purchase orders, records of purchase order requests, expediting records, and reports of shipments received.

These considerations and many others are treated in the following audit programs for the modules related to Inventory Control and Purchasing:

Audit Program: Requirements Planning

1. Review the procedures or other written instruction pertaining to the methods used in the calculation of the numerical requirements of parts and materials.

2. Determine whether calculations of requirements of parts and materials are based on the production schedule and be sure that consideration has been given to quantities on hand, quantities on open order, and quantities needed for production orders previously issued but not yet filled.

3. Determine whether the numerical requirements calculation for an end product (final assembly) is based on:

   ■ Sales order postings
   ■ Management authorized sales forecasts or releases
   ■ Statistical projections of prior usage
   ■ Other (describe)

4. Ascertain whether the numerical requirements calculation for parts and subassemblies is based on:

   ■ An explosion of requirements for final assemblies
   ■ A fixed order point or minimum quantity which is infrequently revised
   ■ A statistical projection of past usage which is revised periodically
   ■ Other (describe)

5. Is a time-phased order-planning system used for material requirements planning?

6. Verify that planned orders at one level (stage) are determined by referring to planned needs for subsequent levels (stages) in production.

7. Review the system for establishing production priorities.

   Outline the system in workpapers and describe the types of priorities.

   Determine the approvals required to authorize priorities.

   Ascertain whether schedule priorities are used primarily to reduce setup interruption.

   Evaluate reasonableness and effectiveness of the system.

8. Verify that changes in product design engineering are quickly reflected in requirements planning.

9. Select a sample of engineering changes (Retrace the adjustments to requirements planning and note any delays).

Audit Program: Inventory Control

1. Review the manual and computerized inventory planning models, and determine whether the models properly allow for product and component interdependencies as well as fluctuations in actual demand and lead time.

2. Is a distinction drawn between independent and dependent demand inventory items?

3. Is the order point technique used only for the independent demand items?

4. If order points are computed, how often are they revised?

5. What type of policy has been established on economic ordering quantities?

6. Determine the technique used in lot-sizing (e.g., economic quantity, discrete lot sizing, or fixed quantity).

7. Does the determination of the economic lot size provide for a balance between ordering and carrying costs? How are these factors taken into account?

8. Verify that records are updated on a timely basis for ordering and planning purposes.

9. Are there controls that assure posting to the perpetual records in a timely basis for:

   Requisitions? Receipts? Customer returns?

10. Age unposted inventory transactions.

11. Verify that ordering rules relate to current conditions.

12. Review ordering rules and perform limited tests of quantities requisitioned.

13. Verify that a follow-up is used to effectively monitor shortages.

14. Review shortage notifications and resultant action taken (re: expediting, etc.).

15. Verify that inventory is stored in an orderly manner.

16. Observe facilities and methods used to store inventory.

17. Verify that a routine procedure is followed to determine obsolete and excess inventory.

18. Review the results of recent obsolescence and excess determinations and ascertain (1) *how* it was done, (2) *what* became obsolete or excess, and (3) *why*, in as much detail as necessary to determine impact on audit program.

19. Is the ABC method or some similar method of classifying inventory by annual dollar value used?

20. Are there written procedures governing management of the various classes?

21. Are separate controls maintained over:
   ■ Consigned merchandise?
   ■ Inventory at outside processors?
   ■ Outside storage (warehouse)?

22. Are all inventories physically counted or confirmed by persons other than stockroom personnel?
   ■ Annually?
   ■ Periodically (cycle counts)?
   ■ Other?

23. Are differences between physical count and perpetual balances investigated?

24. Are perpetual inventory records adjusted to physical counts?

25. If perpetual records are not maintained, is adequate control ensured by:
   ■ Close managerial supervision?
   ■ Frequent review of gross profit percentages?
   ■ Other?

26. Is there a regular review of inventory records and other data to determine quantities on hand which are slow moving, excess, or obsolete?

27. Are these materials stored in a specific area?

28. Is there an active program for disposal of obsolete inventory?

29. Are documented formulas utilized for valuing slow moving, excess, or obsolete inventory?

30. Are material order quantities (and reorder points) computer generated?

31. If material order quantities are *not* computer generated:
    - Are there written reorder point rules?
    - Are there written reorder quantity rules?
    - Are both written reorder point and quantity rules posted on the individual inventory cards?
    - Do the inventory cards show quantities
      a. On hand?
      b. On order?
      c. Allocated?
      d. Available?
    - Are orders placed on the basis of available balances?
    - Are the individual inventory cards controlled?
    - Are physical shortages flagged and investigated?

32. How much of the inventory investment is in work-in-process and components?

33. How do the ratios of these investments relate to cost of sales now, last year, and three years ago?

34. What are the costs of ordering inventory? (For example, these costs might include: setup, stationery, salaries, rent, depreciation, expediting, telephone and telegraph, postage, repairs and maintenance, general administration, etc.)

35. What are the costs of carrying each type of inventory? (For example, these costs might include: depreciation, insurance, interest on investment, rent, supplies, storage costs, obsolescence, protection, taxes, maintenance, salaries, records, etc.)

36. What are the features of the inventory control system which will call near shortages to the attention of the inventory ordering supervisor?

37. Are all items of inventory under perpetual inventory control? What are the exceptions, if any?

38. What type of review has been made of the perpetual inventory system to ensure that it has no unnecessary frills — such as controlling the movements of low priced items which might be controlled more effectively and at less cost by bin-tag or another similar method?

39. Has a continuous inventory verification program been established?

40. What procedure is there for investigating differences between physical inventory counts and the perpetual inventory balance?

41. For inventory replacement ordering, are orders received posted to inventory control records so as to develop that part of the inventory which is available for new orders? If not, how is the sales stock position known?

42. Are safety stocks carried at top level for end products, and bottom level in raw materials to provide:

   - Shelf stock for normal finished product demand?
   - Early ordering of raw material to permit release of manufacturing orders to level production?
   - Reaction to unexpected scrap losses or unusually high finished goods requests?

43. Are unique parts and common parts identified when setting safety stocks?

44. Are items which have lumpy independent demand time phased into the system?

45. Are bills of materials reduced to the minimum number of modules possible?

Audit Program: Material and Component Availability

1. Are schedules or shop orders checked to make certain that materials are available before authorizing the start of production?

2. If component parts and subassemblies are produced, do their production schedules tie in with end-product schedules?

3. Verify that records provide adequate visibility concerning obligated material.

4. Is it necessary to "stage" production in order to determine

whether all parts are on hand or can the formal inventory records be relied upon?

5. If production is "staged" is it "destaged" when the due date is set back?

6. If you utilize a checkout (staging) system, are there written procedures:

   ■ Defining when checkout (or staging) is to take place?
   ■ Limiting checkout to no more than a specified number of days in advance of production?

7. Is there a time limit as to how long material may remain in the checkout (or staging) area?

8. Verify that material staging does not occur too far in advance of production.

9. Perform an aging of staged materials in total, if possible, or on a sample basis otherwise.

10. Are schedules for receiving materials already ordered used for production scheduling?

11. Are shortages hampering production? If so, are they caused by shortages in purchased items or in component parts manufactured by the firm?

12. Determine whether consideration is given to on-hand assembled units and safety stocks before initiating production orders.

    Select a representative number of production orders and compare the quantity to the quantity available at the production order date per Production Control records (See schedule which follows).

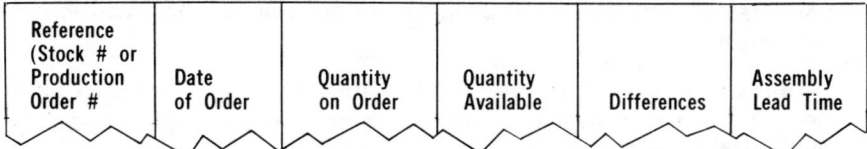

Reference (Stock # or Production Order #	Date of Order	Quantity on Order	Quantity Available	Differences	Assembly Lead Time

Discuss results of review with Production Control supervisors and obtain explanations where consideration apparently was not given to inventory quantities.

13. Ascertain that the status report compares inventory on hand and on order with requirements for ensuing periods and determine that it is:

    ■ Frequent enough for control action
    ■ Issued promptly following the cutoff date
    ■ Used for requisitioning

- Used for expediting
- Used regularly by Accounting for evaluating inventories and reserves

14. Obtain a copy of the format of the status report for reference purposes and include in the work papers.

Audit Program: Purchasing

1. Is up-to-date and accurate vendor or procurement lead time available to production schedulers so that needed parts are on hand and do not cause delay in production?

2. Is lead time given appropriate importance in vendor selection?

3. Under certain conditions, can delivery date supersede quality and price considerations in selecting a vendor?

4. Is the lead time for various inventory items assumed to be relatively constant?

5. Review ordering and receiving dates .for selected materials to determine actual lead times, compute variances between actual lead times and lead times predicted in the inventory planning system, and inquire as to the reasons for variances.

6. Verify that vendor lead times are monitored and changes communicated to production planning as required.

7. Verify that deliveries for volume repetitive items are staggered where appropriate.

8. Review examples of purchase orders requiring staggered deliveries.

9. Verify that an expediting system exists to aid in the timely receipt of materials.

10. Are expediting activities properly coordinated with production scheduling?

11. Does the informal system (or the formal one) attempt to vary lead time according to needs through a system of expediting selected items?

12. Are the formal schedules for receiving materials already ordered accurate and kept current (they and the related production schedules should be revised during lead time to reflect inadvertent changes)?

13. Compare actual receiving dates with expected receiving dates as per the purchase order, inquire about variances, and determine whether changes between expected and actual dates for items on order could have been predicted or otherwise "allowed for."

14. Ascertain whether written guidelines are in effect specifically outlining the procedures to be followed in expediting to assure that it is performed on an organized basis (Review these procedures and comment on their adequacy).

15. Determine whether provision has been made for processing emergency orders.

   Review and comment on the basis used for planning these orders.

   Ascertain whether special expediting techniques are used on these orders and indicate the extent to which these methods may differ from those employed for other orders.

   Ascertain why emergency orders arise and what steps have been taken to reduce or eliminate them.

16. If expediting is excessive, what are the causes and what efforts have been made to eliminate them? (Some causes are: faulty ordering, insufficient calculated lead times used for ordering, paperwork delays, shop overloaded through faults in scheduling, shop refusals to follow schedules)

17. Is there a formal system (or an informal one) for "unexpediting" items not needed either to save expediting costs or to allow for more efficient handling of higher priority items?

18. Review open purchase orders and determine action taken on selected past due items.

19. Verify that appropriate action is taken on critical shortages (line stock-outs).

20. Determine action taken by Purchasing on shortages noted by Production Control.

21. Verify that excess and short shipments are monitored and proper action taken on a timely basis.

22. Review disposition of excess and short shipments with Receiving and Accounts Payable personnel.

23. Verify that users are informed of unreasonable delivery dates.

24. Determine method used to inform users of unreasonable requirement dates.

25. Review recent sales forecast, engineering, and personnel changes received by production planning.

26. Verify that purchase commitment delivery dates and requirements are revised to coincide with major changes in production schedules.

27. Trace the action taken by material control and purchasing with respect to significant changes in the production schedules.

28. Verify that purchase commitments made obsolete by engineering changes are cancelled on a timely basis.

29. Review engineering change orders for past three months and determine action taken by Purchasing where appropriate.

30. Verify that alternate sources are available for critical materials.

31. Secure lists of critical items from Manufacturing and determine sources used by Purchasing.

32. Verify that early and late deliveries are monitored and appropriate action taken on a timely basis.

33. Determine if records of early and late deliveries are kept for vendor rating purposes.

34. Verify that purchase commitments reconcile with current approved requirements.

35. Test selected purchase orders quantities to approved requirements.

36. What procedures are followed to verify quantities of material received? Are purchase items inspected on receipt and noted as accepted or rejected, in whole or in part, on receiving report?

37. What responsibility do Receiving personnel have with respect to returning rejected materials to the vendors?

38. What procedure must Receiving personnel follow in order to accept deliveries which are not in accordance with the purchase orders on file?

39. What procedure must Receiving personnel follow where no purchase order can be located in the Receiving Department?

PRODUCTION SCHEDULING

The discussion in this section focuses upon the modules for Operation Scheduling (K) and Capacity Planning and Loading (J), with lesser emphasis placed on the related modules for Quality Control (L), Manufacturing Cost and Performance Reporting (M), and Maintenance (N). Production Scheduling is responsible for coordinating all of the various production operations. Production scheduling must integrate the work schedules for production departments, assembly lines, and major machines. It also must develop and implement schedules for the procurement of materials.

Scheduling normally is carried out in the context of productive capacity constraints established earlier as a part of production planning. Consequently, scheduling typically accepts the basic plant layout, equipment, processing scheme, and engineering specifications existing in the firm. Within these constraints, production scheduling establishes the timing for all vendor procurements, plant material flows, and production operations.

Internal audits of the Operation Scheduling and Capacity Planning and Loading modules determine the techniques used to set the schedules for procurement and production operations. The audit program reviews all major machine loading and labor planning procedures and determines how machine loads are computed. The program reviews the methods for authorizing production releases to the shop and for maintaining control over the status of work released to the shop. It also tests whether schedule dates are being met, identifies reasons for major discrepancies, and evaluates the techniques used in assigning scheduling priorities to orders.

The modules for Quality Control (L), Manufacturing Cost and Performance Reporting (M), and Maintenance (N) are not a direct part of production planning and control, according to a strict definition. However, assumptions or expectations about material and product quality, labor and machine output rates, and preventive maintenance and repair rates are crucial to all aspects of the production control function. Therefore, a properly conducted audit of that function must test for variances between expected and actual performance in each of these three modules. The firm's procedures for detecting and adapting to significant changes in these areas should be evaluated.

These general considerations are identified in greater detail in the following audit programs for Capacity Planning and Loading, Operation Scheduling, Quality Control, Manufacturing Cost and Performance Reporting, and Maintenance.

Audit Program: Capacity Planning and Loading

1. Have production standards been established to facilitate correct machine loading and to minimize bottlenecks?

2. Does planning predict the workload for each machine in sufficient detail to permit early forecasting of manpower and/or machine priority needs?

3. Have production standards been established to facilitate correct machine loading and the minimizing of bottlenecks?

4. May machines be selected for use regardless of manufacturing cost per unit?

5. Are there problems caused by scheduled work exceeding capacity?

6. Are changes in machine requirements (machine hours per unit)

communicated quickly and accurately to personnel responsible for capacity planning and loading?

7. Once a machine is installed, is there follow-up to see if it performs according to specification?

8. Review records of major additions, replacements, retirements, or breakdowns of machinery, warehousing and shipping facilities; and trace any significant changes to timely adjustments of records and computations of machine availability used in production control.

9. Are machine speeds prescribed to prevent workers from setting their own speeds?

10. Is there extensive idle-labor time?

11. Is there extensive idle-machine time?

12. Are changes in personnel responsible for machine operations reflected in capacity planning and loading?

13. Review a sample of records of employee hirings, terminations, absences, and major reassignments, and trace any significant labor force changes to timely adjustments of records and computations of labor availability used in capacity planning and loading.

14. Are make-or-buy decisions reviewed so that proper consideration is given to purchasing, production, and engineering viewpoints?

15. If *yes*, is the review process structured so that make-or-buy decisions are quickly made?

Audit Program: Operation Scheduling

1. Determine whether the master production plan is the basis for operation scheduling, and compare details of the production plan with the operation schedule for selected items.

2. Determine whether the operation schedule is compatible with the master production plan.

3. Establish that the operation schedule is prepared in writing and is reviewed and approved by an official of the company prior to release to the shop.

4. Are production schedules maintained to the degree of detail and accuracy needed?

5. If *yes*, are the schedules permanently displayed or effectively communicated so that their content is widely comprehended?

6. Ascertain whether subsequent changes follow the same procedure prior to implementation.

7. Retrace revisions of sales order due dates from source documents to resultant revisions in production authorizations.

8. If effective schedules are produced, are they followed and acted on?

9. Are orders completely scheduled by Production Control personnel, or are production foremen required to make many decisions as to routing and/or priority? (Determine whether changes in scheduling are made only by Production Control and not informally by the foremen)

10. Are work assignments normally made with adequate knowledge of order due dates, equipment loads, and operator availability?

11. Are production releases issued on a timely basis?

12. Select a number of shop releases and test to determine that they are compatible with the master production schedule and with the operations schedule.

13. Establish whether formal reconciliations are made to determine major differences between authorized production releases and the master production plan and that such reconciliations are reviewed regularly by officials of the company.

14. Verify that production authorization releases show requirements by model and option where appropriate.

15. Do releases allow for scrap?

16. Are work orders ever started through manufacturing when parts are missing?

17. If *yes*, is Production Control reasonably sure that the missing parts will be received and processed when the rest of the order reaches assembly?

18. Are the lead times used for scheduling reasonable and in accordance with management policy?

19. How and by whom are lead times established:
   ■ On manufactured components?
   ■ On manufactured spares?

20. Has a tabulation been made to determine the variations between actual and forecasted lead times? Does the degree of variation differ materially between different products and suppliers?

21. Compare actual completion dates with scheduled completion dates.

22. Select a sample of recent production items which were completed *after* the scheduled date, and determine the reason for any discrepancies.

23. How are overruns or shortruns controlled? What causes them?

24. How many items were short last month, as compared with the prior month, last year and three years ago?

25. What type of expediting procedure exists for speeding up production of near-shortages to avoid shortages?

26. Is there a machine load prepared for production scheduling and, if so, on what basis is it prepared?

27. What safeguards exist so that workloads and personnel requirements will be scheduled far enough in advance for the shop to plan work force and machines, thus balancing capabilities against requirements?

28. To what extent is the following information developed for use of Production Control and manufacturing floor supervision:

    ■ Charts for daily review of the delivery schedule?
    ■ Monthly reports, showing status, performance, predictions, and release data for each product, product family or other basis for scheduling production?
    ■ Monthly or more frequent status reports showing what items will be short if not received before the beginning of the next production cycle?
    ■ Critical machine parts and weekly machining performance reports?

29. Does Production Control check the accuracy of its records?

30. Appraise the adequacy of the system by which Production Control maintains control of the status of production activities.

31. Select a representative number of actual requests for production, and to the extent practicable, check the quality and timing of actions relative to the:

    ■ Basis of origin of the production request
    ■ Manner of acceptance by the Production Department
    ■ Determination of needed inputs
    ■ Transmittal of requests for needed inputs
    ■ Receipt and testing (where required) of inputs
    ■ Determination of machines to be used and related internal actions
    ■ Dissemination of internal production instructions
    ■ Production of specified products

48

- Inspection
- Release of products

32. Establish whether machine loading techniques are centralized for overall control or whether they are informal to the point that the foreman schedules work through his area; describe and evaluate methods used.

33. Determine whether workloads are planned far enough in advance so that machine and manpower capacities are balanced to requirements.

   Establish whether problems exist with schedule exceeding capacity.

   Review overtime premium paid to determine whether substantial amounts are paid; relate overtime premium paid to idle time and machine utilization reports to see if premium was justified.

   Establish by review of the time records whether there is any extensive idle-labor time.

   By review of machine utilization reports ascertain whether there is any extensive idle-machine time.

   If any of the production lines comprise machines whose running speeds are not uniform, ascertain that this is contemplated when scheduling workloads.

   How far is scheduling affected by the prior months' backlog? Is this formally rescheduled or does the foreman take care of it?

34. Is information about changes in material and availability of components effectively used to adapt the operations schedule?

35. Are changes in parts and subassembly production schedules communicated quickly, accurately, and reliably?

36. Is the operations schedule properly adapted for changes in machine capacities?

37. Is the operations schedule properly adapted for relevant changes in production personnel?

38. Are any changes which are relevant to the operations schedule also reflected in expediting (or unexpediting) activities?

39. Is the priorities planning system operating effectively?

40. If two or more orders are received and one must be delayed, is there a formal system for determining which job has priority? Is there an informal communication network to determine these priorities?

41. Select a number of sales orders or bills of materials which are provided to Production Control on the same date; retrace the marketing request to the resulting responses in inventory and production planning; evaluate the priorities implied by such responses.

42. Can the progress of any job be checked readily? If a delay is encountered, is it communicated to the departments affected on a timely basis?

43. Review the method of status reporting employed to report the progress of an order through the shop.

 Describe the nature of the techniques employed.

 Evaluate whether the system provides data on all orders and not merely those of a critical nature.

 Select a random sample of orders and verify that they are actually located in the areas indicated on the status report.

 Check whether control records are posted daily for the previous day's activity.

 Review the controls employed to assure that all production counts are reported to and posted by Production Control.

 Comment on whether the status reports appear reasonably accurate and promptly indicate schedule slippage.

44. Determine the status of open production orders by selecting a sample of open production orders from the files and comparing the required production dates with the audit date.

45. By review of status reports, observation, and subsequent discussion with appropriate supervision, ascertain whether there are any significant accumulations of incomplete assemblies being held up in process due to:

 ■ Parts shortages
 ■ Starting work ahead of schedule or without schedule reference
 ■ Inspection holdups
 ■ Repairs and replacements of defective components
 ■ Equipment and/or manpower overloads at next station
 ■ Improper identification and routing
 ■ Machine breakdown (establish causes)

46. Determine whether setup breaks or downtime present significant problems:

 Do cases frequently arise when the time between the start and completion of an order in production could be reduced by splitting lot sizes and moving materials to the next operation station more frequently?

Select a representative number of closed production orders and determine the ratio of setup time and downtime to running time (the following schedule will be helpful).

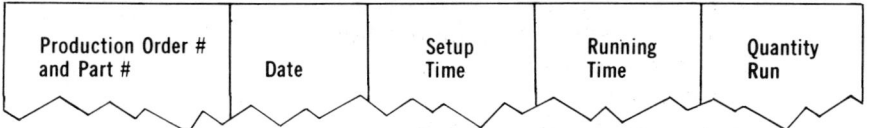

Production Order # and Part #	Setup Time	Down-time	Running Time	Quantity Run	Ratio of Setup Time to Running Time	Ratio of Downtime to Running Time

Through discussion, establish a desirable ratio of setup time to running time for the items involved above and compare to the actual ratio calculated. (Discuss with appropriate supervision where significant variances exist.)

Compare actual downtime with the tolerances established by Engineering and investigate major differences. (Are these reported to management by Production Control?)

Select several major parts and determine the frequency of their production within a representative period and setup time required, using the following schedule:

Production Order # and Part #	Date	Setup Time	Running Time	Quantity Run

Where numerous setups are incurred for the part numbers selected above, discuss the possibilities and limitations of computing economic order quantities.

47. Where reports and observations indicate lack of machine availability, determine whether problems exist relative to machine bottlenecks. (Review the routines followed in resolving machine overload and comment on their adequacy)

48. Are requirements for common parts consolidated into schedules so that there is no undue repetition of setups for production of the same items?

Audit Program: Quality Control

1. Is there a need for quality control in the company?

2. If *yes*, is there such a program?

3. Are reports that permit the prompt identification of quality problems and the taking of timely corrective action prepared?

4. Are there established procedures for control of defective or damaged goods received?

5. Are major quality control problems communicated to Engineering for analysis of whether bills of material or labor standards should be revised?

6. Review major quality control reject items and determine that major quality control variances are analyzed.

7. Is there a formal procedure for inspecting returned products?

8. Is there a measurement of the cost of the Quality Control Department?

Audit Program: Manufacturing Cost and Performance Reporting

1. Is actual production compared with planned production and are deviations noted?

2. Select a sample of recently closed production orders and determine the following:

	Number
Orders completed a month or more late	_____
Orders completed a week or more but less than a month late	_____
Orders completed less than a week late	_____
Orders completed on schedule	_____
Orders completed early	_____
Total tested	_____

Analyze and evaluate the reasons production orders are completed late or early.

Trace the production orders sampled to the appropriate customer orders to establish whether customer delivery reflects a similar pattern.

Where customer orders are to be delivered late, determine whether the system provides for early notification to the Sales Department so that contact can be made with the customer regarding the delinquency. (Such timely action may eliminate cancellations by customers or, where product differentials are minor, permit the sale of substitute items)

Ascertain the extent to which late deliveries will result in:

a. Fines

b. Premium freights

c. Changes of shipping schedules to foreign countries

d. Exchange losses caused by deferred collection of foreign exchange

Where customer orders are delivered early, ascertain the extent to which special arrangements have been made to deliver the merchandise early and to collect the receivable in line with the accelerated delivery date as opposed to the originally scheduled delivery date.

3. Determine whether departures from preferred routing are appropriately controlled.

Indicate and evaluate the level of authority required to approve alternative routings.

Test a representative number of manufacturing process sheets to determine that alternative routings are properly approved.

Based on the sample in item 2 of this list, calculate the total cost incurred through use of alternative routings, and compare to the cost of preferred routings. (*Note:* Alternative routings usually result in more costly production)

Determine whether consideration was given to possible higher costs when the alternative routing was selected. (Obtain explanations for the actions taken)

Determine why departures from preferred routings occur and what steps have been taken to avoid recurrence.

4. Using the following schedule, test a representative sample of production orders to establish that effective control is maintained over quantities produced in the consecutive steps of the manufacturing process:

| | | Quantities of Parts | | |
Production Order # or Date	Department or Operation	Received	Reported as Produced & Forwarded	Differences

Reconcile the differences noted, giving consideration to:

The quantity provided for scrap, rework, or salvage in specifying the quantity to be produced

The type of records maintained for parts pulled off the line and follow-up procedures employed. (Ensure that the system prevents the substitution of good parts for spoiled ones)

The relationship with the quantities produced in successive departments

Whether parts inventories are properly controlled so that workers will not be able to secure new parts to replace spoiled parts or to perform unauthorized rework

5. Appraise the reporting system as it applies to the various parts of the production operations at the various levels of supervision, with particular reference to:

- Scope
- Adequacy of variance analysis
- Timing or release
- Focus on controllable costs
- Persons to whom directed
- Degree of summarization

6. Is information available to management on the utilization and efficiency of machines and manpower by department?

7. Does management take action to raise efficiency when the figures show deficient utilization (total potential hours versus actual hours used)?

8. Does Accounting give Manufacturing the costs by product on a monthly basis?

9. Is reporting adequate; that is, are reports accurate and prepared early enough for corrective action by the right people?

10. Are manufacturing reports actually used by management?

11. Are idle-time reports prepared for machines and men? Do they contain the reasons for idleness?

12. Are employees' capabilities matched to the task when necessary?

13. Are there formal procedures for recording excess labor, computing its cost, and minimizing it?

14. Do labor scheduling techniques permit timely reaction to changes in production schedules?

15. Are there enough direct labor time codes to cover all machine situations?

16. Is there a need for management to improve time recording accuracy and responsibility? (If so, prepare a separate schedule)

17. Is information available to management on the utilization and efficiency of machines?

18. Does each machine critical to sustained output have a backup operator?

19. Is a record of scrapped items maintained?

20. If *yes*, is this record used to measure the effectiveness of the supervisor, to measure the effectiveness of employees, to determine cost to the company, and to serve as a guide in reducing its cost?

21. Are scrapped parts replaced by a requisition that is approved by the department foreman and reviewed later by the manufacturing manager?

22. Is the generation of scrap reported to Production Control? Operation scheduling?

23. Does the work order system provide documents for cost control of job progress, machine repair records, and closeout control completion?

24. Do computer programs for standard costs of materials, labor and machine usage use the same standards as are used in bills of material for production planning?

25. Are these further analyzed to determine whether the production standards or bills of material need revision?

26. What are the bases for recent schedule changes in the various manufacturing areas?

Audit Program: Maintenance

1. Was the system of preventive maintenance in force designed to avoid machine breakdowns affecting production? Is it effective and economical? Is maintenance performed during the production lines' non-working hours?

2. Are major deviations from expected machine breakdowns incorporated into revised engineering standards?

4 EPILOGUE: HOW TO PREPARE AND PLAN FOR FUTURE AUDITS OF PRODUCTION CONTROL

Many firms are not presently involved in operational audits of production control but plan to conduct such audits in the near future. The planning and preparing for a future initial audit of production control require careful attention. What preparatory steps should the auditor take before attempting to conduct the production control audit?

The first step should be to become thoroughly familiar with the basic production control concepts and procedures. The production control publications listed in the bibliography should prove helpful in this. A reading of either the Buffa (1973) text or the Plossl and Wight (1967) text would help provide this basic background.

Second, the auditor should become familiar with recently developed concepts, procedures, and systems (e.g., the material requirements planning (MRP) approach) designed to adapt the basic concepts and procedures to obtain an effective, adaptive control system in a dynamic, rapidly changing environment. An excellent presentation of these recent approaches is offered in the book by Wight, *Production and Inventory Management in the Computer Age* (1974). Also see Appendix B.

The third step requires auditors to become thoroughly familiar with their own firm's production control system. The internal auditor should talk in-depth with various personnel related to production control, including marketing and sales forecasters, customer order processors, product design and manufacturing engineers, inventory control managers, purchasers, expediters, requirements planners, schedulers, maintenance supervisors, production managers, and production control supervisors. The auditor should tour the production facilities and observe actual operations of each function. These should provide the auditor with a good overview of specific procedures, documents, interactions, and problems of the firm's production control system.

Fourth, the auditor should attempt to learn about the operations of production control systems used in other firms. This can broaden and improve the auditor's basis for developing standards of performance and for making suggestions for improvements. Participation in educational programs, seminars, and presentations on production control; discussions with production control and related personnel; reviews of procedures, documents, and approaches; and even observations of actual operations of production control systems of other firms will greatly enhance the auditor's general understanding of production control. As a result, the quality and effectiveness of the audit should improve significantly.

The final step in planning and preparing for the production control audit is for auditors to merge their understanding of production control systems with their expertise in operational auditing in order to develop specific audit programs.

This monograph is designed as a guide in this process. It discussed the basic concepts and procedures of production control (Chapter 2 and Appendix B), analyzed the implications of these concepts and procedures for internal operational audits of adherence control and adaptive control systems (Chapter 2), and suggested operational audit programs (Chapter 3). It is designed as an overview to be read by the auditor at the start of the process of planning for a future audit of production control and as a basic reference for the final selection of procedures to be used in audit programs for various portions of the production control function.

SURVEY OF INTERNAL AUDITORS[1]

GENERAL BACKGROUND[2]

1. *To what specfic unit in your company's organizational structure are you assigned?*

   I am assigned to:
   The Internal Auditing Department   [70]
   Another department   [2]
   An individual manager or officer (vice president, plant manager, production control manager, etc.)   [8]
   Other   [5]

   This unit is:
   At the corporate level in the organizational structure   [65]
   At the divisional level in the organizational structure   [8]
   At the operating department level in the organizational structure   [2]
   Other   [2]

2. *How is the internal auditing function structured in your company? (Check as many as apply.)*

   We have a formal Internal Auditing Department at the corporate level.   [70]

   We have formal Internal Auditing departments at the divisional level.   [13]

   We have formal Internal Auditing departments at less than divisional level (i.e., at each plant location, etc.).   [3]

---

[1] The sample selection process is discussed in Chapter 1. A narrative summary of the responses is presented at the end of Appendix A.

[2] The number of respondents indicating a particular answer is shown in the bracket to the right of each item.

We have internal auditors assigned to corporate offices but have not established a formal Internal Auditing Department at the corporate level. [0]

We have internal auditors assigned to divisions but have not established formal Internal Auditing departments at the divisional level. [5]

We have internal auditors assigned to less than divisional organized units (i.e., operating departments, plant locations) but have not established formal Internal Auditing departments at these levels. [3]

Other. [11]

3. *What are the requirements for employment as an internal auditor in your company? (Check as many as apply.)*
Must be a CPA [11]
Graduate degree [12]
College degree in accounting [41]
College degree with a specified major other than accounting [20]
Any college degree [13]
Some college work [2]
High School graduate [4]
Corporate accounting experience [18]
Internal auditing experience [27]
Public accounting experience [18]
Diversity in technical backgrounds [11]
Other experience [10]
Other [7]

4. *How frequently are your schedules of audits normally developed?*
Annually [62]
Quarterly [13]
Monthly [12]
Weekly [1]
Whenever existing audits are nearing completion [5]
Other [8]

5. *Are you familiar with the procedures used by your company to forecast demand?*
Yes [53]
No [22] (skip to question 16)

6. *What procedures does your institution employ to forecast demand? (Check as many as apply.)*

Executive judgment based primarily on a percentage increase or decrease compared to last year's operations [16]

Jury of executive opinions involving independent estimates from a broad range of executives who then communicate with each other to reconcile differences and arrive at the final forecast [20]

Top-down approach — estimating total demand (i.e., gross national product) then breaking it down to industry estimates, then company estimates, and then product line estimates, etc. [19]

Grass-roots approach — asking the smallest knowledgeable components (i.e., each salesman to estimate demand for their area, then submitting the estimates to the next higher echelon for revision and summary, etc., until the forecast is revised by the final authority [22]

Other [12]

7. *What are the time horizons for the forecasts employed by your company? (Check as many as apply.)*

Less than one year [26]
One year [41]
Two through four years [11]
Five years [40]
Six years [1]
Seven to nine years [2]
Ten years [11]
More than ten years [4]
Don't know [0]

8. *How detailed are your forecasts?*

Total demand for the company only [1]
Breakdown of the company's demand by general components such as by divisions [24]
Breakdown of the company's demand by product or service being offered [43]
Other [2]

9. *How accurate have the forecasts been in the past year at corporate level?*

Generally within [0-20%] of actual demand

10. *Are forecasts regularly compared to actual results?*
Yes [54]
No [2]
Don't know [0]

If yes, are large deviations from the forecast investigated?
Yes [52]
No [1]
Don't know [0]

11. *Approximately how often does your company update its forecasts?*

Type of Forecast	Frequency
Annual	Monthly to quarterly
Intermediate term (2-4 years)	Annually
Long term (5 years or more)	Annually

12. *Does Internal Auditing participate in either developing the forecasts or auditing their implementation?*
Yes — developing [1]
Yes — auditing the implementation [13]
Yes — both [2]
No [39]
Don't know [0]

PRODUCTION PROCESS CONTROL AND PLANNING

13. *Approximately what percentage of your specific unit's time is spent in audits of production control in any area?*

0% [13]
1-10% [6]
11-20% [9]
21-30% [3]
More than 30% [3]
Unable to estimate [17]

The following questions refer to the production control areas which your specific unit audits. If you audit more than one production control area, please select the unit that you are most knowledgeable about and apply your answers to it.

14. *How would you describe the production process which your specific unit audits?*
Mostly continuous processing [27]
Mostly job shops [10]
About half and half [6]
Unable to estimate [2]
Other [3]

15. *To what extent does the year-to-year sales demand for these products vary?*
Extremely variable [5]
Considerably variable [16]
Generally stable [23]
Very stable [1]

16. This question omitted due to inconclusive results.

17. *Is the production control function:*
a separate department from the specific production department it serves? [34]
integrated into the specific production department it serves? [23]
other? [6]

18. *What specifications or requirements does your Production Control Department consider in establishing production schedules?*
Company standards and specifications [42]
Customer specifications [37]
Government requirements (national) [29]
Government requirements (state) [17]
Government requirements (local) [12]
Independent standards (i.e., Underwriters Laboratories, etc.) [16]
Material requirements [37]
Labor requirements [34]
Machine requirements [29]
Plant engineering requirements [21]
Quality control requirements [31]
Production control requirements [27]
Other [6]
Don't know [6]

19. *What organizational components are consulted by Production Control in establishing production schedules?*

Accounting [16]

Internal Auditing [3]

Manufacturing [56]

Marketing/Sales [53]

Plant Engineering [27]

Process Engineering [31]

Quality Control [24]

Other [8]

20. *Does Production Control have written procedures to control:*
    A. Production scheduling dates?
    Yes [32]   No [20]   Don't know [8]
    B. Machine loadings?   Yes [27]   No [21]   Don't know [8]
    C. Production capacities?
    Yes [28]   No [20]   Don't know [11]
    D. Scheduling lead time?
    Yes [33]   No [15]   Don't know [8]
    E. Expedited work?   Yes [25]   No [18]   Don't know [12]

21. *If yes, to any of the above (otherwise skip to question 22), which of these procedures are:*
    Audited by both Production Control and Internal Auditing?
    A [14]   B [10]   C [10]   D [15]   F [9]
    Audit by Production Control only?
    A [18]   B [14]   C [14]   D [13]   E [11]
    Audited by Internal Auditing only?
    A [6]   B [2]   C [2]   D [4]   E [6]
    Not audited by either?
    A [2]   B [6]   C [1]   D [3]   E [3]

22. *Are written procedures established to determine:*
    A. When to order materials?
    Yes [34]   No [16]   Don't know [6]
    B. How much materials to order?
    Yes [34]   No [16]   Don't know [6]
    C. If materials are obsolete or slow moving?
    Yes [33]   No [16]   Don't know [6]
    D. If materials are overstocked?
    Yes [33]   No [16]   Don't know [9]

23. *If yes to any of the above (otherwise skip to question 24), which of these procedures are:*

Audited by both Production Control and Internal Auditing? (Circle as many as apply.)
A [20]   B [21]   C [23]   D [18]

Audited by Production Control only? (Circle as many as apply.)
A [6]   B [4]   C [5]   D [7]

Audited by Internal Auditing only? (Circle as many as apply.)
A [9]   B [12]   C [13]   D [13]

Not audited by either? (Circle as many as apply.)
A [1]   B [1]   C [1]   D [2]

24. *Who is primarily responsible for determining whether production control procedures (both written and verbal) are adhered to by Manufacturing?*

Internal Auditing   [10]
Production Control   [47]
Other   [11]

25. *To what extent is Production Control computerized?*

Processes are actually connected to the computer and are controlled by it on line as the product is being produced.   [12]

Process data are fed into computers, and reports are issued on a regular basis.   [36]

Computers are occasionally used to solve specific problems.   [9]

Computers are rarely used in the production control area.   [14]

Other   [3]

26. *To what extent is the computer utilized in internal audits of production control?*

Extensively   [4]
Occasionally   [16]
Rarely   [16]
Never   [22]

27. *Does Internal Auditing audit the following?*

Inventory safeguarding Yes [60] No [2]
Forecasted demand Yes [12] No [45]
Production planning Yes [25] No [29]
Production scheduling Yes [25] No [32]
Implementation of production plans and schedules.
Yes [25]   No [31]

28. *What percentage of the internal audits of production control is spent in auditing the following areas?*

	0-20%	21-80%	81-100%
Inventory safeguarding	[17]	[10]	[10]
Forecasted demand	[9]	[0]	[0]
Production planning	[13]	[3]	[0]
Production scheduling	[13]	[1]	[0]
Implementation of pro- duction plans and schedules	[11]	[1]	[0]

29. *In what sequence were these audits first undertaken by Internal Auditing? (implemented first, second, etc.)*
Inventory safeguarding (Generally listed as *first*)
Forecasted demand (Generally listed as *fourth* or *fifth*)
Production planning (Generally listed as *second*)
Production scheduling (Generally listed as *third*)
Implementation of production plans and schedules (Generally listed as *fourth* or *fifth*)

FUTURE AUDITING PLANS

30. *Does your specific unit intend to audit the following activities, procedures, or specifications within the next two years?*
Sales forecast procedures
Yes [21] No [25] Don't know [6]
Some production control activities
Yes [45] No [7] Don't know [5]
Company standards and specifications
Yes [23] No [11] Don't know [4]
Independent standards (i.e., Underwriters Laboratories)
Yes [2] No [40] Don't know [8]
Materials requirements
Yes [39] No [7] Don't know [2]
Labor requirements
Yes [32] No [16] Don't know [5]
Machine requirements
Yes [20] No [24] Don't know [8]
Plant engineering requirements
Yes [14] No [30] Don't know [8]
Quality control requirements
Yes [26] No [20] Don't know [7]
Production scheduling
Yes [36] No [13] Don't know [6]

Machine loadings
Yes [13]　No [30]　Don't know [7]

Production capacities
Yes [17]　No [28]　Don't know [7]

Scheduling lead time
Yes [22]　No [21]　Don't know [8]

Expedited work
Yes [18]　No [23]　Don't know [11]

Inventory safeguarding
Yes [53]　No [2]　Don't know [2]

Implementation of production plans and schedules
Yes [33]　No [14]　Don't know [7]

Occupational Safety Hazards Act (OSHA)
Yes [24]　No [19]　Don't know [9]

Other
Yes [2]　No [3]　Don't know [2]

May we have a copy of audit programs used in these areas?
Yes [6]　No [35]

31. *To what extent has internal auditing of production control in your company changed in the last five years?*
Extensively　[11]
Moderately　[24]
Very little　[26]

32. *How important is each of the following factors in developing your schedule of internal audits of production control?*

	Very Important	Important	Unimportant	Not Considered
Requests from top management	[37]	[17]	[3]	[0]
Requests from the managers of the operations to be audited	[15]	[39]	[3]	[0]
Determined by the audit staff to provide a comprehensive coverage	[23]	[31]	[0]	[2]
Determined by the audit staff to investigate specific problem areas	[21]	[29]	[3]	[1]

33. *In what ways has internal auditing of production control in your company changed in the last five years?*

Selected responses to this open-ended question were used in the preparation of the text.

34. *What plans have been formulated to either begin or extend internal auditing of production control?*

Selected responses to this open-ended question were used in the preparation of the text.

NARRATIVE SUMMARY OF SURVEY RESPONSES

The questionnaires were answered primarily by internal auditors assigned to a formal Internal Auditing Department at the corporate level in the organizational structure.

In these firms, sales forecasts reportedly were developed by different methods. No method was predominant. Forecasts appeared to be generated on both a long-term basis (generally longer than one year) and a short-term basis (generally one year or shorter).

These forecasts provided a starting point for production scheduling and, as such, were disaggregated into demand by division and by product within the division. The forecasts were updated periodically, and actual customer orders were checked regularly against the forecasts.

Generally, these forecasts were accurate within 0-20% of actual demand. Large deviations from the forecast were investigated, but it is interesting to note that internal auditors were involved in auditing the implementation of sales forecasts in only approximately 25% of the firms that responded.

The production process reported in the survey involved primarily continuous processing. Approximately 25% were job shops. There was a mixture of both stable and fluctuating sales-demand situations among the respondents. Production situations included both those where custom goods were made to order and where standard goods were manufactured to maintain standard inventory levels.

Some respondents indicated that the production control function was integrated into the specific production department it served and others indicated that Production Control existed as a department separate from Production. Approximately 60% were reported as being separate departments.

In order to coordinate production activities, the Production Control departments reportedly considered numerous specifications and requirements and consulted with most functional areas in the firm, especially the production and marketing functions.

Approximately 60% of the firms responding to the survey had

written procedures to control production scheduling, lead time, and operating performance. Internal auditors were involved primarily in audits of production scheduling and of purchasing lead time.

Written procedures were common in determining order quantities, order points, obsolescence, and overstocking of materials. Internal auditors were heavily involved in auditing these areas. In general, internal auditors were more heavily involved in areas that dealt with inventory considerations.

Although inventory was the primary focal point of the internal auditor, future audit plans reportedly were being expanded to include most of the procedures, specifications, and activities associated with production control. Results also indicated that audits of production control activities are being included more frequently in audit plans.

Appendix B

CONCEPTUAL OVERVIEW OF PRODUCTION CONTROL

The efficient production of any product requires that effort be expended to bring together the right combination of materials, manpower, and machines at the right time.

Figure B.1 illustrates the flow of physical resources for the production of a single product requiring several processes in each of several stages of production. The illustration is greatly simplified because it involves only a *single* product and because there is only *one* use for the output of each process; i.e., it is used in a single process at a subsequent stage.

The first process of the first stage of an *m* stage production system required the availability of (1) sufficient quantities of suitable kinds and qualities of material; (2) sufficient quantities of labor capable of operating machinery, moving materials, and supervising operations; and (3) the proper equipment.

Production control may be thought of as a process that plans and controls flows into and out of *reservoirs* of the three major categories of resources: materials, labor, and equipment.

The materials reservoir is the inventory of raw materials or component parts available at any point in time. The flow from this reservoir into the production process is governed by the bill of materials, which specifies the quantities and types of materials (as well as labor and machine capacity) needed for each stage of production of a specified product. The flows into the materials reservoir are from receipts of raw materials from vendors.

These inflows are affected by purchasing policies and procedures, by vendor lead time, and by such inventory policies as safety stock and economic order quantity. If the materials reservoir is too small, insufficient materials will be available for production needs, resulting in production delays and possible customer dissatisfaction. If the materials reservoir is too large, excessive carrying costs will be incurred in the form of warehousing costs, insurance, and interest on inventory investment.

If instantaneous replenishments of the materials reservoir were possible because of zero lead time consumed in processing orders

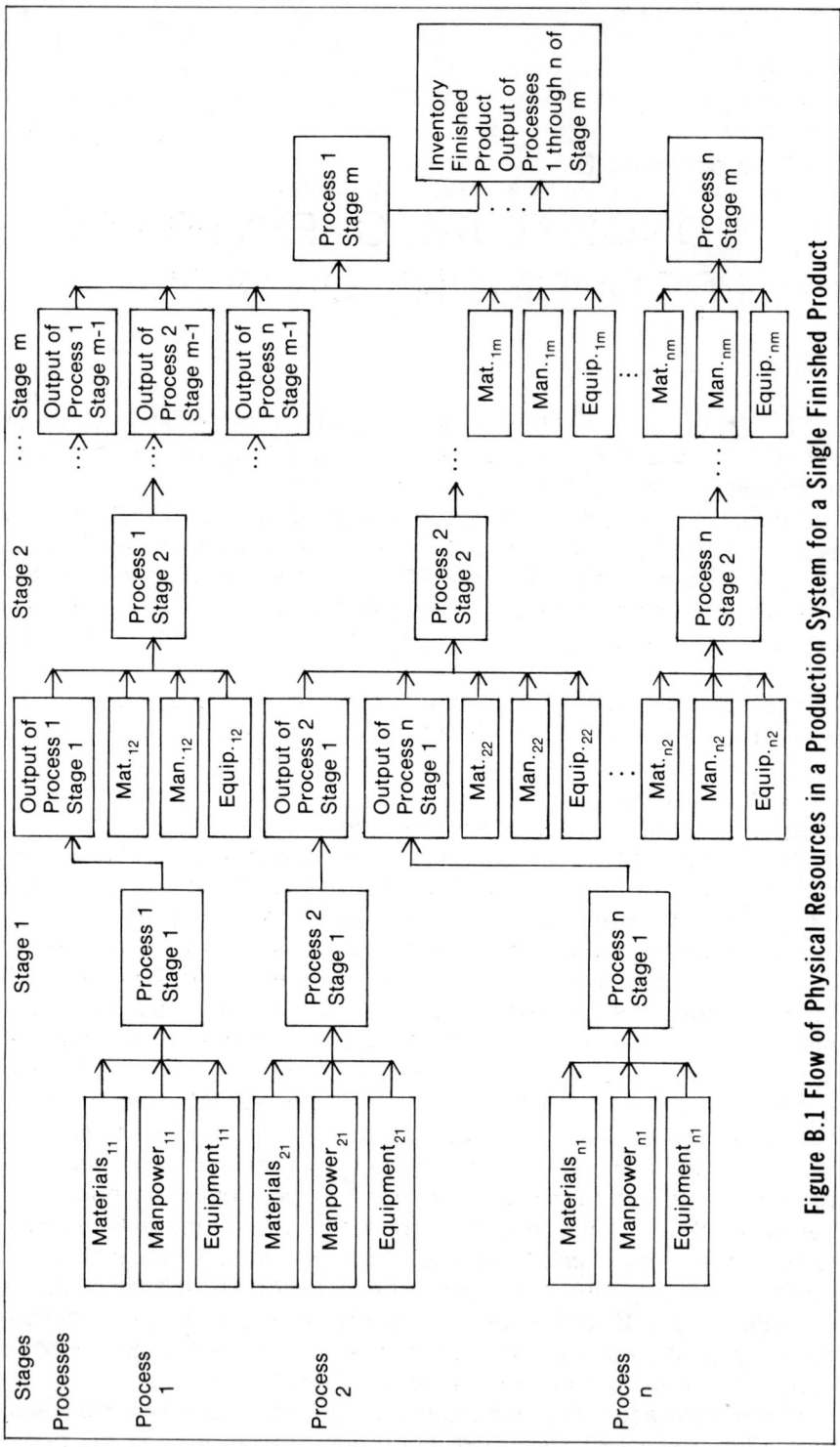

Figure B.1 Flow of Physical Resources in a Production System for a Single Finished Product

and obtaining materials from vendors, the reservoir could be deleted without resultant production delays and poor service to customers. However, in most practical applications, lead time is not zero and, therefore, significant consideration is required in inventory and production control decisions.

The labor force at a given time can be viewed as a manpower reservoir with a constant outflow representing the total hours worked during a period. The outflow is constant since labor hours, unlike materials, cannot be kept in inventory for future use. The labor outflow requirements for a given product are specified in the bill of materials. Available labor time not productively used can be viewed as a flow of manpower into idle or wasted time.

The size of the reservoir (or flow) is affected by the personnel policies of the firm, especially with respect to hiring and training. If specialized skills are required for a given production process, any increase in the reservoir (flow) of suitable manpower required by current production needs would be subject to lead time delays associated with hiring specialized personnel and/or training them to perform the specialized tasks. In highly specialized production processes, this lead time can be considerable.

The machine reservoir (flow) is similar to the manpower reservoir in the sense that outflows for a given reservoir level (labor force or machine capacity) are determined by the passage of time. The outflow during a period is the total available hours of different types of machinery and equipment for that period. Since these hours cannot be placed in inventory, hours of outflow not productively used will result in either downtime because of repairs, setup time to prepare for a new production run, or idle time because of scheduling slack. Additional hours of machine time needed in the reservoir will be subject to lead-time delays associated with procuring additional equipment and incorporating and balancing this equipment into the line by Manufacturing Engineering.

As noted, different functions are associated with the three reservoirs. The purchasing function is concerned with the material reservoir. The personnel function is concerned with the manpower reservoir, and the manufacturing engineering function is concerned with the machine reservoir.

These reservoirs, of course, do not exist in isolation but are closely interrelated. Thus, the production processes can be constrained by a lower level in one reservoir, even though the other reservoirs are in an overflow condition. It is a basic objective of Production Control to coordinate with the functions of purchasing, personnel, and manufacturing engineering, among others, to provide a balance in the three reservoirs and, thus, a smooth flow of production output.

The output of one or more processes will often be used along with other materials, labor, and machines in another process at a later stage. For example, the output of the first process of stage 1 is used in the first process of stage 2. The outputs of processes 2 through *n* of stage 1 are used in the second process of stage 2. In this situation, the coordination of some processes (e.g., processes 1 and 2 of stage 2) is interrelated with the coordination processes at precedent and subsequent stages (stages 1 and 3).

The planning process for the production of the final product in Figure B.1 requires a series of steps which begins with a plan for the number of units of the final product to be produced, and proceeds backward from plans for the final stage (stage *m*) to successively earlier stages — all the way back to stage 1, the earliest stage in the production process.

The basis for this planning process is the product bill of materials, which is normally developed by product design engineers and which specifies the materials, labor, and machines required at each stage of production.

A CONCEPTUAL VIEW OF PRODUCTION CONTROL SYSTEMS

An enlightening conceptual analysis of the interaction among the production system, other organizational systems, and environmental systems was developed by Buffa (1963) and is discussed below (see Figure B.2).

The production system is viewed as a subsystem within the total organizational (firm) system. This is, in turn, a subsystem within the total environmental system. The purpose of the production system is to transform production ingredients into finished products. The major organization subsystems related to the production subsystem are the policy-formulating system, the control system, and intermediate organization systems.

The policy-formulating subsystem has as its major function the establishment and subsequent modification of major organizational policies. These policies are established in response to information about the environment and about organizational operations. This information is provided by the control systems, by feedback from the intermediate organization systems, and by subjective (intuitive) information developed by policymakers from a variety of other sources.

The policy-formulating system has line authority to establish high-level policies. It involves value judgments as well as questions of political power, the formation of coalitions, organizational conflict, and other interpersonal behavioral dynamics. This system exists at high management levels where the objectives and policies of the company are set.

The control system has as its basic function the processing and transmission of information. The "analysis," "forecasting," and

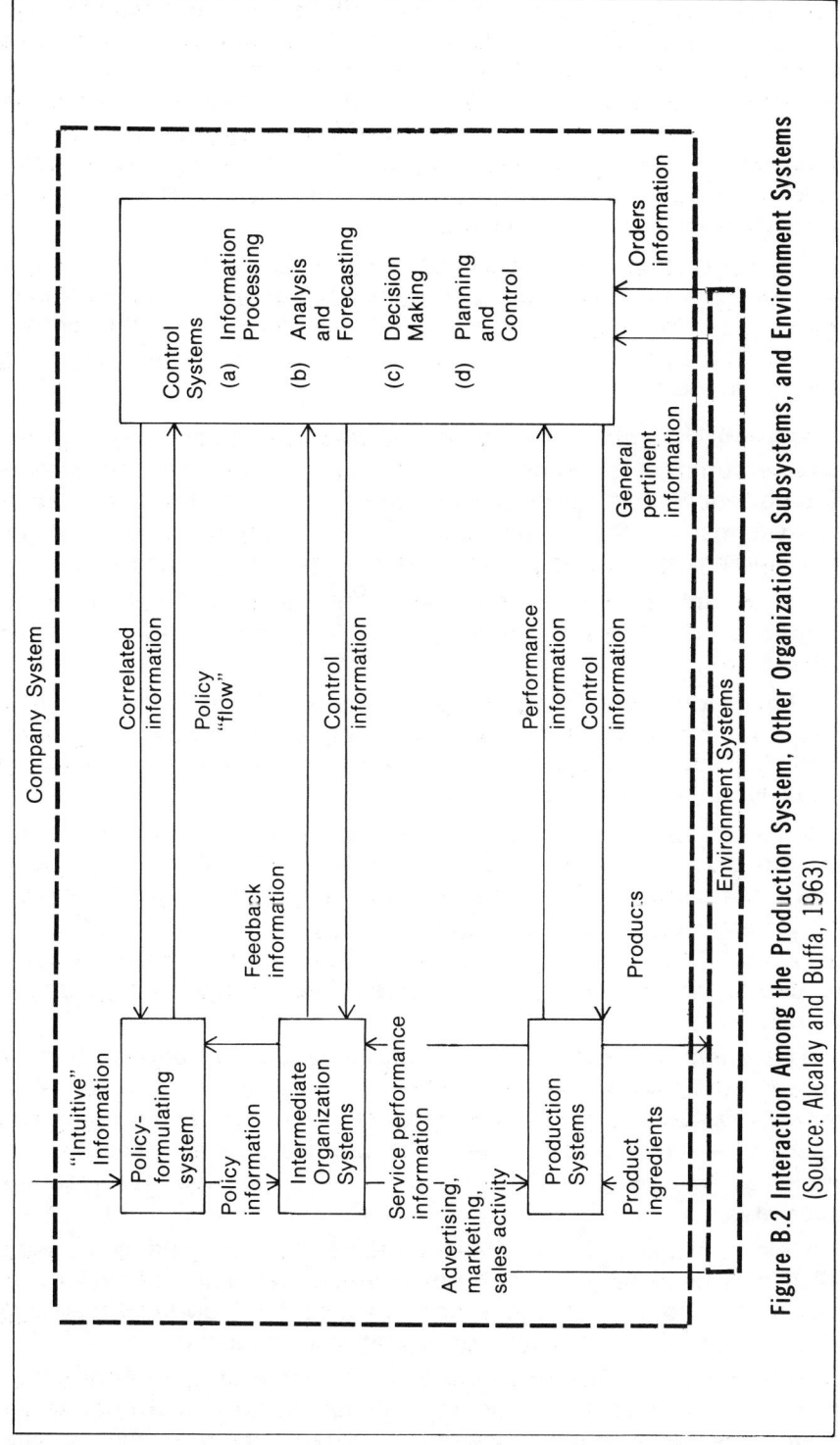

Figure B.2 Interaction Among the Production System, Other Organizational Subsystems, and Environment Systems
(Source: Alcalay and Buffa, 1963)

73

"decision making" shown in Figure B.2 could be accomplished entirely on the basis of prescribed analytic and decision models which process specified information inputs according to a predetermined format and merely identify the analytic or decision "output" which is prescribed for that combination of inputs by the policymakers or higher-level programmers. Most control systems have not reached this level of sophistication and, therefore, involve a good deal of human judgment.

Control systems most often act in a staff function rather than in a line-authority function. The goal of the control systems is to process information in such a manner that the policies of the policy-formulating system are implemented. Production control is such a control system.

The intermediate organization systems are viewed as having the service function of supervising, delegating authority, and trans-mitting decisions concerning the interface between other subsystems in the organization or the same system in the environment that directly affects the organization subsystem.

These intermediate organization subsystems include such functions as finance, personnel, purchasing, marketing, and engineering.

The production control system in this framework exists as a planning and control function that correlates the production system with the other functions of the firm in an effort to meet the objectives set by top management.

A closer look at the relationship between the production system and the control subsystem is shown in Figure B.3. The only physical flows are shown as the flow of ingredients (materials, manpower, and machines) into the production system and the outflow of products. The remaining flows are all information flows — some related to control feedback and some related to communications of policy.

The effective operation of a productive system requires that an appropriate system be established to measure (1) the standard ingredients necessary for each product, (2) the actual reservoirs and flows of each ingredient, and (3) the lead times necessary to replenish inventory or to adapt the level of the labor or machine capacity.

Communicating these measurements via the data processing system is necessary not only for low-level feedback of signals for day-to-day control of operations but also for high-level feedback signals necessary to adapt organizational systems.

The operation of an optimum control system requires information from several sources, including forecasted and actual information about the environment, incoming orders, major organizational

74

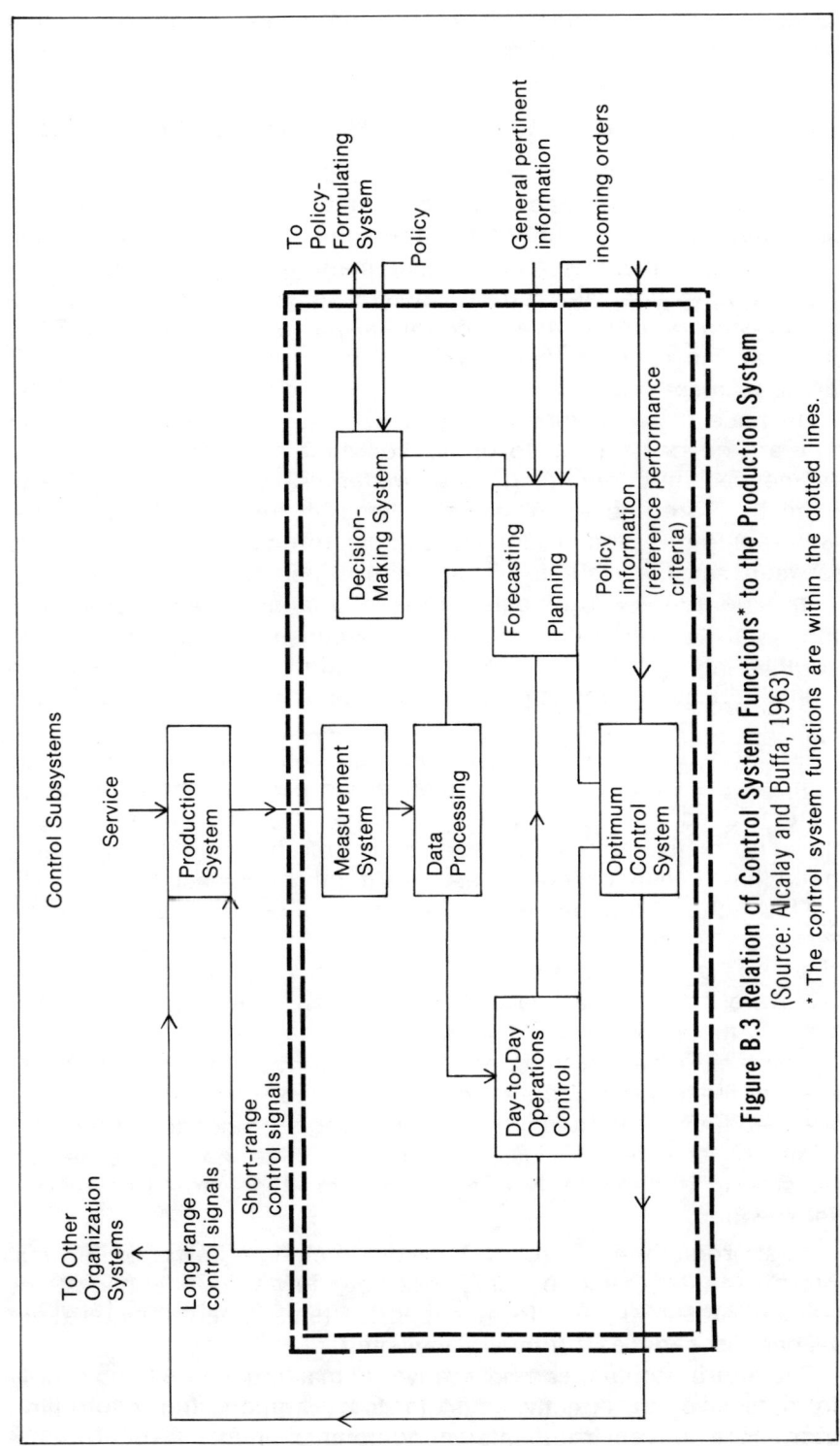

Figure B.3 Relation of Control System Functions* to the Production System
(Source: Alcalay and Buffa, 1963)

* The control system functions are within the dotted lines.

75

policies, and day-to-day control of production operations. This is the role of production control.

PRODUCTION CONTROL IN A CHANGING ENVIRONMENT

If the environmental factors related to sales demand and manufacturing were stable and predictable with a high degree of certainty, production control would be a relatively easy task, even in a complex multistage, multiproduct manufacturing situation.

From a practical view, production control is usually fraught with a multitude of interdependent, continually changing variables. Such changes can cause difficult production control problems such as failing to meet production due dates, producing some items too far in advance of when they are needed, producing some items after they are needed, failing to obtain some materials by the time they are needed, and obtaining other materials too far in advance of when they are needed. These problems, in turn, can cause havoc with attempts to plan production and can bring about bitter conflicts between sales, production, and finance personnel.

In general, these problems represent a failure to adequately plan and control production priorities. Because of inadequacies in communicating the most relevant production control information on a timely basis, inadequate attention is given to high priority items and too much attention is given to lower priority items.

Production of a critical product is often delayed because all components except one are available and because the information system failed to detect its unavailability far enough in advance to allow corrective action. Indeed, some of the other components might have been expedited at considerable expense.

This action, of course, is wasted when one or more of the necessary components to complete the product is unavailable. When a given component in a multicomponent product is discovered to be unavailable at a specified time, the need for the other components is correspondingly delayed.

However, many production control information systems fail to account for this rescheduling of the expected "need" date, resulting in expediting components that will no longer be needed at the time originally specified. Thus, considerable time and expense are invested in unnecessarily expediting items that should have been unexpedited.

Most production control systems provide either formal or informal information to expedite items, but very few information systems provide timely signals to unexpedite items when they are not needed as early as originally expected.

The entire problem can be neatly summarized: many firms simply do not have an effective system for planning and controlling priorities when environmental conditions change.

PLANNING PRIORITIES AND PLANNING CAPACITIES

One of the leaders in developing practical production control systems that effectively adapt to rapid, complex environmental changes, Oliver Wight (1974, p. 11), identifies four primary functions of a production control system:

- Planning priorities

- Planning capacities

- Controlling priorities

- Controlling capacities

Wight correctly maintains that the key to a properly functioning, adaptive production control system is the *planning of priorities.* If a firm does not know what components are needed and when they are needed — the essence of priorities planning — it cannot effectively plan the required capacity.

Furthermore, effective control is necessarily dependent upon effective planning, whether priorities or capacities. Therefore, it follows that the cornerstone for the proper operation of these four basic production control functions is priorities planning.

Figure B.1 displays some of the complexities which are typical in modern multistage production processes, even when only one finished product is manufactured. It provides insight concerning why effective adaptive control is so difficult to attain and why it necessarily relies upon the proper functioning of a system of planning priorities. The finished product in Figure B.1 could be produced to fulfill an existing specific customer order or to be held in inventory to meet an anticipated future demand. If the product can readily be standardized to meet the varied requirements of numerous customers, it will usually be manufactured for inventory. However, if the requirements of customers are so diverse as to make standardization impractical, the product will be made-to-order in accordance with the customer's unique specifications.

Let us consider the problems of priorities planning for a made-to-order, multistage product with the interrelationships of processes and stages shown in Figure B.1.

First, when an order for a custom product to meet unique customer specifications is received or contemplated, the firm's product design engineers will need to develop a bill of materials.

The bill of materials should include information very similar to that in Figure B.1. It specifies the various stages and processes as well as the materials, manpower, and machines necessary to make the product.

The process of estimating a delivery date and of scheduling production requires a careful planning of production priorities. The firm must decide exactly what, how much, and when the ingredients of production are needed.

Let us consider a production system in which there are three sequential stages with several processes which can be conducted simultaneously within each stage. Each process requires one week to complete. Here, the need for materials in the third and final stage of production is time-dependent upon the outputs of the second stage. This is, in turn, time-dependent upon the outputs of the first stage.

It would take a minimum of three weeks to complete the item. In order to complete production in three weeks, materials to be used in the third stage must be available by the beginning of the third week.

If third-stage material is neither in inventory nor on order and if the normal lead time without expediting is five weeks, Production Control faces two options relative to planning priorities: Either the completion date must be delayed by three weeks, or the materials must be expedited. If expediting could cut the lead time from five to three weeks, the firm could avoid delaying the completion date because of this item.

Therefore, expediting the procurement of this third-stage material and setting a three-week completion date for production would appear to be justified.

If, however, material used in the first stage is currently neither in stock nor on order and if lead time for procuring the material is three weeks with a strong expediting effort (four weeks without expediting), the product completion date cannot be earlier than six weeks. In this case, there would be no need to expedite the third-stage material. However, the third-stage material might have been expedited before the delay in the first-stage material was discovered. In this case, the information system should trigger the *unexpediting* of the third-stage material before additional expediting costs are incurred.

Consider another element in this case. Process 2 of Stage 2 might have been originally scheduled for completion at the end of the second week; and the delayed availability of the first stage material, say Material $_{11}$, might have been discovered after the original scheduling. If the production control information system fails to adapt completely to the new information, it would show a two-week completion date for Stage 2 Process 2. However, the output of this process would not be needed until the beginning of the sixth week. This is a problem of planning and controlling priorities.

In the absence of complete adaptive control feedback information, attention will be devoted to the priority of completing Process 2 of Stage 2 by the end of the second week — quite likely at the expense of a more critical production priority — even though a three-week delay would have no adverse effects on opportunity costs.

An effectively operating adaptive system of planning and controlling production priorities should have shown that the production factors to be used in Process 2 of Stage 2 during the second week were actually available for alternative production activities, where delays might have resulted in significant opportunity costs.

TYPICAL ADAPTIVE CONTROL PROBLEMS

The complexity of these interrelationships focuses upon three important problems: (1) the inadequacy of informal adaptive systems, (2) the misinformation contained in the so-called "expedite lists" or "hot lists," and (3) the inappropriateness of standard economic order quantity (EOQ) inventory models. These are discussed below.

Inadequacy of Informal Attempts at Adaptive Control

In many firms, a problem arises when the formal production control system fails to communicate accurate, reliable, and comprehensive information regarding the complete set of adaptive changes necessitated by an unexpected change in some factor. The production control system continues to produce data, but it is inaccurate and unreliable.

This may occur whenever a customer's required delivery date changes, a required inventory item is discovered missing, an expected lead time for procuring a component part changes, a critical employee (e.g., machine operator) is absent or incapacitated, a required material or product fails to pass quality controls, a required machine breaks down, or another critical factor of production changes.

Most often, when this happens, an informal production control system arises that allows employees, particularly production people, to adjust for information that they believe is inaccurate. Unfortunately, the informal system can also generate incorrect responses. In fact, this is generally the case.

The problem is not that an informal system exists. Most companies have such a system to complement the formal system and can benefit from its flexibility. The problem occurs when the informal system largely replaces the formal system as the major production control system and is causing production problems. These production problems usually entail missed production due dates and unnecessary buildups of inventory.

In many cases, a formal production control system does not have the necessary flexibility to react quickly to the numerous changes demanded of it. A great number of information flows are required for a formal production control system to adapt effectively to changing conditions. Consequently, many systems, especially manual systems, can be swamped in a quagmire of paperwork.

In this situation, an informal production control system often arises and communicates these changes between key individuals in the system without the necessity of the corresponding paper flow. For example, a salesperson may learn that a customer will need an item at an earlier date than was originally specified. Rather than prepare the paperwork required by the formal system, the salesperson simply may tell the production supervisor who may assign a higher priority to the item.

Another common occurrence is that sales personnel build slack into their delivery date estimates. When production people believe that certain due dates are "softer" than others, they may reduce the priority assigned to these items by the formal production control system.

In the previous example using Figure B.1, an attempt at informal adaptive control may occur when it is discovered that Material$_{11}$ will be delayed by two weeks.

Here, the production foreman may decide that, since the first process of the second stage will necessarily be delayed by two weeks, all the other second-stage processes could also be delayed by two weeks without adversely affecting the product completion date. He may informally approve the delays in these other processes of the second stage by giving priority to other production items.

This would result in a discrepancy between the formal system, which shows these second-stage processes as being late (an undesirable condition), and the informal system which regards the shift in priorities as desirable adaptation.

The informal system can often work quite effectively to overcome the limitations of the formal system — at least for a limited period of time. However, several factors can erode the effectiveness of the informal system.

One factor is the exploding complexity of the system. The system may reach the point where it is so complex that individuals cannot informally communicate all the necessary information with the required degree of accuracy and reliability.

A second factor may occur when personnel who were essential to the effectiveness of the informal system are replaced through retirement or transfer. An informal system, to be effective, usually requires that the individual members be both knowledgeable and experienced.

A third factor arises when role conflicts are not quickly resolved and become intense enough to effectively destroy the free exchange of required information, especially between marketing, engineering, and production personnel.

For example, the conflict between a salesperson's objective of satisfying the delivery request of a particular customer and the production manager's objective of minimizing inventory and production change (start-up) costs may lead the salesperson to deliberately distort the information needed for a smoothly operated production control system.

By falsely stating an earlier due date, the salesperson may meet an immediate, short-run objective but only at the expense of a smooth operation of the production control system as a whole.

What faces many managements, therefore, is an informal production control system that produces inaccurate responses. The basic problem, however, is that the formal production control system is not sufficiently adaptable to change.

Expedite Lists and Hot Lists Are Misleading

One sign of a nonadaptive production control system is an excessive proportion of orders appearing on expedite lists. When expedite lists become too lengthy, it is impossible for the expediter to give top priority and attention to every item on the list.

As a result, a kind of superlevel expedite list is developed — often informally — to identify those "hot list" items which are more critical than the average expedite items.

Even this second level of "hot list" expedite items is often allowed to grow to an unmanageable level in many firms.

An investigation of a sample of items on the expedite or hot lists would probably reveal that a significant proportion of the items should have been unexpedited because other factors in the production process had eliminated the need to have the item on the date specified on the expedite list. Consequently, the expedite list information is often unreliable and misleading.

EOQ Models Are Often Inappropriate

Many firms use the standard economic order quantity (EOQ) models to determine when and how much inventory to order. Such models appear to be appropriate for determining the *quantity* of materials to order, but they are quite inappropriate for determining *when* to order (the reorder point), especially in an interdependent multistage production system.

The reorder point formula used with most EOQ applications follows:

Reorder Point = (Number of Days of Lead Time) × (Average Daily Usage) + (Safety Stock)

Material may have a lead time of 20 days, an average usage of 30 units per day, and a safety stock of 300. The material should then be reordered when the inventory gets down to 900 units [(20 × 30) + 300 = 900]. This formula involves a computed factor and a judgmental factor.

The judgmental factor involves estimating what should be the safety stock — a determination which receives no guidance from the formula but which may potentially be adjusted for unexpected changes in lead time or demand.

The computational factor in the formula is inadequate for a dynamic system. It involves assumptions that both demand and lead time are (1) constant, (2) known with certainty, and (3) independent exogenous variables. The effect is that, whenever demand or lead times diverge from the mean estimate, the formula is inappropriate except to the extent that human judgment can compensate for inadequacies in the formula.

If the need for one material is completely independent of other materials and components, the EOQ formula may operate relatively well. However, when the complex interdependence of contemporary production systems is introduced, EOQ models may become quite dysfunctional. In Figure B.1, there are three interdependent stages of production.

The EOQ reorder point is often unreliable when applied to dependent demand items.

For example, the use of an EOQ model may have a 95% reliability. This would result in the deletion of safety stock only 5% of the time within each process.

If three processes are sequentially connected, the probability of at least one of the three processes being out of stock — thus resulting in a delayed product completion date — would be about 14% ($1 - .95^3 = .1426$) instead of 5%.

If there are ten interdependent sequential processes, each with a reliability of .95, the probability of a delay in production would be about 40% ($1 - .95^{10} = .4012634$).

Consequently, the EOQ reorder point method becomes unreliable for dependent demand items.

THE MATERIAL REQUIREMENTS PLANNING APPROACH

Because of the inappropriateness of the EOQ models for interdependent materials, many firms use a time-phased method of determining inventory order points. This method is commonly designated material requirements planning (MRP).

The basic concept of such a method is that the demand for items (material requirements) in later (subsequent) stages of the production sequence becomes the basis for material requirements at earlier (preceding) stages. A central element of such a system is a bill of materials which clearly and accurately details the materials (as well as labor and machines) needed at each stage.

One of the leading proponents of the materials requirements planning (MRP) approach, Oliver Wight (1974), explains the application of the time-phased order technique in the context of manufacturing a bicycle.

Material requirements planning for three stages (levels) of production sequence are considered: the bicycle itself, the

1. First Level: Master Schedule for Bicycles

Weeks	1	2	3	4	5	6	7	8	9	10	11	12
Bicycles	40	0	50	0	0	60	0	60	0		80	0

2. Second Level: MRP — Handlebars
Lead Time = 4; Order Quantity = 100

		1	2	3	4	5	6	7	8	9	10	11	12
Projected Requirements		40	0	50	0	0	60	0	60	0	40	80	0
Scheduled Receipts				100									
On Hand	60	20	20	70	70	70	10	10	-50	-50	-50	-130	-130
Planned Order Release					100			100					

3. Third Level: MRP — Cut Tubing
Lead Time = 5; Order Quantity = 200

		1	2	3	4	5	6	7	8	9	10	11	12
Projected Requirements					100			100				160*	
Scheduled Receipts													
On Hand	140	140	140	140	40	40	40	-60	-60	-60	-60	-220	-220
Planned Order Release			200				200						

* Requirements from another handlebar for another bicycle.

Figure B.4 Time-Dependent Order Schedules

handlebar component, and the cut tubing used for the handlebars (Figure B.4).

The master schedule shows production of 40 bicycles in week one, 50 in week three, 60 in weeks six and eight, and 80 in week 11. The MRP schedule for handlebars is based upon the master schedule for bicycles and the bill of materials.

At the beginning of the planning period, 60 handlebars are on hand; and 100 units are already on order and expected to be delivered in week three. In the absence of planned order releases (requiring a lead time of four weeks), there will be a negative balance of 50 in week eight, changing to a negative balance of 130 in week eleven.

To cover these potential negative balances, orders will have to be released in weeks four and seven. The number of units ordered is determined by the standard order quantity, perhaps based upon the EOQ formula.

Projected requirements for cut tubing amount to 100 in week four, 100 in week seven, and 160 (for another handlebar on another bicycle) in week eleven to satisfy the planned order releases for the handlebar manufacturing process. A planned order release at one stage (level) of production determines the projected requirements for preceding stages. Anticipated negative balances amount to 60 in week seven and 220 in week eleven. Since there is a five-week lead time and an order quantity of 200, orders to manufacture the cut lengths of tubing should be released in weeks two and six.

If the standard reorder point formula is used in situations such as this, it will mean that the order for the material will quite often be released either too late or too early. If the order is released too late, the result is usually a production delay. When the order is released too early, the result will usually be either excessive inventory buildup or needless expediting.

The MRP technique, since it is designed for dependent demand items in inventory, has far greater applicability than the reorder point formula technique. However, the production control literature, as a whole, fails to recognize this. Wight explains this discrepancy as follows:

Book after book has been written on inventory management without ever mentioning MRP. The order point always got the attention. Undoubtedly, the biggest reason for this was the fact that, during the 1960's, there was a great fad for sophistication. Anything nonmathematical like MRP was looked upon as being quite pedestrian. Statistical concepts could be used with the order point technique; and thus it received most attention from the college professors, most of the consultants, the operations research and management science people, and, consequently, many of the data processing systems people. It has been observed that, for many years, the amount of literature on statistical order point versus MRP and the application potential for the techniques seemed to be inversely related. (Wight, 1974, p. 31)

One of the most significant advantages of the MRP technique is that goods cannot only be expedited easily but unexpedited easily as soon as it is discovered that they are no longer needed on the original due date. This, of course, makes expediting of the remaining critical items much easier. In this way, priorities can actually be planned and controlled.

The suggested planning horizon for MRP is a *minimum of one year.* Shorter planning horizons than a year for final product demand do not permit sufficient time to effectively allow for cumulative lead times required at various sequential stages of production.

Plans and schedules should be detailed to weekly (or shorter) periods. Monthly or quarterly information would simply not be precise enough for effective priorities planning. Monthly reports would not provide much guidance to expediters regarding which items are most important for immediate attention.

The planned order release in MRP also provides considerable assistance for effectively planning machine loading and adjusting capacities. The basis for machine loading and capacity planning is the authorization of production release (see the Operation Scheduling module of Figure 2.3). If a manufacturing line manager is given sufficient advance notice of future production releases, he or she will be in a much better position to efficiently plan appropriate capacity adjustments. The MRP system, if it is properly implemented, will provide planned order releases which do this on a regular, accurate, and reliable basis.

The essence of MRP is that it incorporates the adaptive features of informal systems — which are characteristically inaccurate, incomplete, and unreliable — into a formal system with features designed to make it practical, adaptive, reliable, accurate, and relatively complete. Some of the features of MRP are better expressed by Wight as follows:

It is important to recognize that MRP is really just a formalization of the informal system. Consider a company making an assembled product. The expediter goes to the stockroom with the bill of material for the product that appears in the master schedule. He checks to see if the material is available. He frequently pulls this off the shelf and "accumulates" or "stages it," putting it on a pallet and then making up a shortage list. He will then expedite those parts that appear on the shortage list.

The computer, in effect, is simply doing the same thing using MRP. It takes a master schedule, looks up the bill of material in its own files to find out what material is required to manufacture the product in the schedule, and then checks the inventory to see if this material is on hand. If the materials are not on hand, it tells the planner to order it and tells him when it will be needed. If the material is already on order, it will reevaluate the due dates on that material and tell the planner if the due dates need to be changed. MRP is really simply a formal system for predicting the shortages that simulates what the expediter was really trying to do. (Wight, 1974, pp. 38-39)

An effective, adaptive control system will monitor all of the relevant production control variables (see Figure 2.3) for significant changes. Whenever a significant change occurs in any such variable, reliable and accurate data about the change should be inputted at the appropriate point in the production control information system.

For example, any significant increases in material rejections because of failure to meet quality control standards should be analyzed in an effort to determine whether the increases are likely to continue. If they are expected to continue, product design engineers should be informed so they can adjust the standard bill of materials for the item.

Likewise, any significant changes in labor variances or machine breakdowns must be quickly and accurately detected and analyzed. If they are expected to continue, manufacturing engineering should be informed so that labor standards, routings, and machine loadings can be revised.

An effectively operated MRP system will allow the production control system to respond to these changes on a reliable, accurate, and timely basis.

BIBLIOGRAPHY

Alcalay, Jack A., and Buffa, Elwood S. "A Proposal for a General Model of a Production System." ed. Elwood S. Buffa. *Readings in Production and Operations Management.* New York: John Wiley & Sons, Inc., 1966, pp. 36-52.

Buffa, Elwood S. *Modern Production Management.* 4th ed. New York: John Wiley & Sons, Inc., 1973.

Buffa, Elwood S. *Operations Management: Problems and Models.* 3rd ed. New York: John Wiley & Sons, Inc., 1972.

Buffa, Elwood S. *Readings in Production and Operations Management.* New York: John Wiley & Sons, Inc., 1966.

Cadmus, Bradford. *Operational Auditing Handbook.* Altamonte Springs, FL: The Institute of Internal Auditors, 1964.

Greene, James H. *Production and Inventory Control Handbook.* New York: McGraw-Hill Book Company, 1970.

Lindberg, Roy A., and Cohn, Theodore. *Operations Auditing.* New York: American Management Association, Inc., 1972.

Mautz, R. K., and Sharaf, Hussein A. *The Philosophy of Auditing.* American Accounting Association Monograph No. 6. Sarasota, FL: American Accounting Association, 1961.

Plossl, G. W., and Wight, O. W. *Production and Inventory Control: Principles and Techniques.* Englewood Cliffs, New Jersey: Prentice-Hall, Inc., 1967.

Sawyer, Lawrence. *The Practice of Modern Internal Auditing.* Altamonte Springs, FL: The Institute of Internal Auditors, 1973.

Skinner, R. M., and Anderson, R. J. *Analytical Auditing: An Outline of the Flow Chart Approach to Audits.* New York: Pitman Publishing Corporation, 1966.

The Institute of Internal Auditors. *Statement of Responsibilities of the Internal Auditor.* Altamonte Springs, FL: The Institute of Internal Auditors, 1971.

The Institute of Internal Auditors. *Internal Audits of Inventory Control and Management.* Research Committee Report 16. Altamonte Springs, FL: The Institute of Internal Auditors, 1970.

The Institute of Internal Auditors. *The Internal Auditors Review of Organizational Control.* Research Committee Report 18. Altamonte Springs, FL: The Institute of Internal Auditors, 1972.

Wight, Oliver. *Production and Inventory Management in the Computer Age.* Boston: Cahners Publishing Company, Inc., 1974.

Wilson, Paul W. *Internal Audit Manual.* National Retail Merchants Association, Controllers Congress, 1969.